AF423859

CHOOSING HAPPINESS

Choosing Happiness

A Study of the Beatitudes

DANIELIA WILLIAMS-BOSTEDO

Blessed with Truth Ministsries

Copyright © 2023 by Danielia Williams-Bostedo

All rights reserved. No part of this book may be reproduced in any manner whatsoever without written permission except in the case of brief quotations embodied in critical articles and reviews.

First Printing, 2023

CONTENTS

~ 8 ~

Blessed are the persecuted for righteousness' sake

~ 8 ~

Part I (Continued)

~ 8 ~

Part II: Biblical Example

~ 8 ~

Part II: Biblical Example

~ 8 ~

Part III: Personal Example

~ 8 ~

Part IV: Go Deeper

~ 9 ~

Psychology and Happiness

Footnotes

INTRODUCTION

Everyone wants to be happy. Happiness is even in the Declaration of Independence—We have a right to the pursuit of happiness. However, where does happiness come from? Why does it seem so much further and further away from the average person today?

The Bible has something to say about happiness. God uses the word blessed. Blessed means supremely happy, spiritually prosperous, finding favor. The Bible says "**Happy** is the man that findeth wisdom, and the man that getteth understanding. For the merchandise of it is better than the merchandise of silver, and the gain thereof than fine gold. She is more precious than rubies: and all the things thou canst desire are not to be compared unto her. Length of days is in her right hand; and in her left hand riches and honour. Her ways are ways of pleasantness, and all her paths are peace. She is a tree of life to them that lay hold upon her: and **happy** is every one that retaineth her. (Proverbs 3:13-16)

Our society, too, has something to say about happiness. It is to be pleased or content. Audrey Hepburn said "The most important thing is to enjoy your life—to be **happy**—is all that matters." Kim Kardashian said "**Happiness** is my family..." Bo Derek said "Whoever said that money can't buy **happiness**, simply didn't know where to go shopping." Taylor Swift said "The truth of the matter is **happiness** isn't a constant. You get fleeting glimpses of it, when the rest of it, you're fighting for those moments."

What is your definition of happiness? Do you think it's regularly attainable? Is it brought by something so trivial as money? Is it found in our families? Is it all that matters? You may have a combination of thoughts about happiness, but one thing is for sure: You want happiness!

Our lives have developed a worldview of what happiness is and how we can have it. The Bible, however, is unchanging. It has nothing to do with my life, per se, or yours. It is the same no matter who we are or where we are from or how much money we have. So, I find my answers in God's Word, which I can count on. I challenge you to hear and seek from God's Word—challenge yourself.

Would you say that people today are pleased or content in their lives, generally speaking? Does it seem like we just can't find happiness? We are always looking to what is next, rushing this chapter of life to go on to the next. We lose sight of what we have, always wishing for more. This doesn't bring happiness. In fact, even in those times that we do get more, we aren't satisfied. We then lose sight of that and want even more. "He that loveth silver shall not be satisfied with silver; nor he that loveth abundance with increase: this is also vanity." (Ecclesiastes 5:10)

God has always known this. His answer is to turn to Him...turn to His Word for Truth and wisdom, which bring happiness. "**Happy** is he that hath the God of Jacob for his help, whose hope is in the LORD his God:" (Psalm 146:5); "**Happy** is the man that findeth wisdom, and the man that getteth understanding." (Proverbs 3:13); "...and whosoever trusteth in the LORD, **happy** is he." (Proverbs 16:20)

I will tell you that I found the Word of God to be very challenging. It goes against the nature of everything that I was and thought that life was. As I began to study the Word of God, I questioned a lot, and you will too; however, don't give up because you have questions. Don't give up because you don't understand everything. Truth is, we will never understand everything that God tells us, but little by little, He will shed light on His truth, and it will become valuable to us and we will see happiness—true happiness—stir in our lives.

We will study the Beatitudes, part of the Sermon on the Mount, the greatest sermon by the greatest preacher—that preacher being Jesus Christ. Every Be-Attitude begins with "Blessed" or "Happy." You might be thinking, "Yes, what do I need to do to be happy?" I mean, that is the way that we are taught. There are hundreds of books that have a step-by-step approach to how you can be happy, but God tells us that we must not DO; we must BE. He doesn't give us things to do that we might be happy. He tells us that ***our happiness is in our position.***

Again, it doesn't make sense to our natural mind, but God teaches the inner man—the spirit. It is His Spirit that teaches our spirit, and if we do not have the Spirit of God, these things are impossible to understand. "But the natural man receiveth not the things of the Spirit of God: for they are foolishness unto him: neither can he know them, because they are spiritually discerned." (1 Corinthians 2:14) Yet, still, people have used Biblical truths to guide their lives for centuries, and that is good, but how much better when it is more than just principles but life-changing attitudes because of our position in God!

Without the Spirit of God, you can learn from this devotional book. You will learn of attitudes that will be beneficial to you in your life. But, with the Spirit of God, you will be taught in ways that my words cannot teach. You will be deeply affected in your spirit and will be given the power to live out these unique, life-changing attitudes and experience true happiness.

$$\sim I \sim$$

BLESSED ARE THE POOR IN SPIRIT

Part I—INSIGHT (What does this mean?)

"Blessed are the poor in spirit: for theirs is the kingdom of heaven." (Matthew 5:3)

To be poor in spirit one must be humble—recognize your low estate. God promises something greater than we can imagine. He is the Creator. He is the One who holds life in His hands, and He wants to have a relationship with all people. He wants His kingdom to be our kingdom—the kingdom of heaven.

Humility or to be humble is not something that our society is fond of. In fact, like many of the attitudes of Christ, the world sees them as a weakness. One thing that is often confused with humility is that people think it means to *think less about yourself,* but it means to *think about yourself less.* As you will see through this study, it is never God's will that we beat ourselves up, even when we go against Him. His position is always one of love, mercy, and restoration.

The Bible says that we will be divinely favored or supremely happy if we would be poor in spirit. It is an attitude—a choice. The Beatitudes should not be confused with how to be saved, although this first one is needed to be saved. The other Beatitudes only build on this one. After all, our God is orderly.

Nobody gets saved without realizing that they need a Savior—realizing that I want something that I can't get on my own. See, everybody wants to go to heaven, if they think about it, but we can't get to heaven on our own. Everybody wants to be happy, but we will not be happy without God. We can pretend, but generally the "so-called" happiest people in our world (as you look on the outside) are the most drug-addicted and depressed people. Just look at Hollywood actors, singers and overall wealthy people and the suicide rate and drug overdose rate within those demographics. It's extremely high. Why? Because money can't buy happiness. Looks like Bo Derek was wrong in the quote mentioned earlier.

We all want love, yet we find our experiences with others to be lacking the fulfillment of that love. We lack peace and unity. We live in fear and disappointment, and we want different.

We need a Savior—One to deliver us! We must realize that we cannot get these things on our own, and all the idols in the world (money, success, relationships, tv, drugs, religion...etc.,) cannot fill what God has created for Himself to fill.

This is not just a one-time realization that we are poor in spirit—that we are destitute of the things that we desire most. Daily, I must choose to realize that I NEED God. How can I do that? For me, it started because I took that first step and was humble, recognizing that I needed love. I needed Jesus. Then, I accepted Him, and the kingdom of heaven became mine.

Now, my outlook is different. This is not my home. These things here on earth, including my feelings, are temporal. They fade away, but God and all that He is for me and through me is eternal. His Word and what He has taught me is eternal. The influence that I can have in the lives of others is eternal, lasting forever! I am blessed!

There is an opposite attitude to the attitude of humility and that is the attitude of pride. Pride is having a high view of yourself—"an unreasonable conceit of one's own superiority in talents, beauty, wealth, accomplishments, rank or elevation in office, which manifests itself in lofty airs, distance, reserve, and often in contempt of others."[1]

Unfortunately, this attitude is embraced by our society, but it is an attitude that brings ruin. The Bible warns: "Pride goeth before destruction, and an haughty spirit before a fall." (Proverbs 16:18) As seen in the Websters 1828 dictionary definition of pride, pride often becomes hateful toward others. When we think that we have achieved more than others or that we are more beautiful than others or that we are just better than other people (which is what pride says), we will treat people terribly, and we will not be happy with bad relationships. In fact, we will be miserable.

Being the best athlete on the team, the smartest student in the class or the brightest associate in the office will make you feel good for a while; however, it is the attitude of feeling the best that will eventually push people away from you.

With the attitude of pride, you will not see the need for a Savior. You will believe that you have enough, did enough, and are good enough to make it to heaven or that you don't even need heaven. Pride, unfortunately, divides people and sends people to hell.

While this is an acceptable stance in America today, the kingdom of God is different. With God there are no ranks. The pastor is not more important to God than the five-year-old girl that just got saved today. Therefore, God calls for humility. Even though you are the best on the team or the smartest in the class, with humility you can help others around you and lift them up because of your talents. That is the desire of God: that the things that He blesses us with will bring us closer to others—not push others away.

"A man's pride shall bring him low: but honour shall uphold the humble in spirit." (Proverbs 29:23) Pride does not lead to happiness but humility does; therefore, we can choose to think about ourselves less, understanding that there are some essential things that we NEED that Jesus can provide, and this is the first attitude that Jesus mentions will bring us true happiness.

~ 1 ~

PART II: BIBLICAL EXAMPLE

"Blessed are the poor in spirit, for theirs is the kingdom of heaven." (Matthew 5:3)

I can think of no better example of poor in spirit than Jesus, Himself. He was 100% God and 100% man, and though He had the power and authority of God, He also had the weakness and temptation of humanity.

He chose to be poor. He chose to let Himself be 100% in surrender to God the Father. He showed us what humility and respect look like. "Let this mind be in you, which was also in Christ Jesus: Who, being in the form of God, thought it not robbery to be equal with God: But made himself of no reputation, and took upon Him the form of a servant, and was made in the likeness of men: And being found in fashion as a man, He humbled himself, and became obedient unto death, even the death of the cross. (Philippians 2:5-8)

Poor in spirit—to be humble—to make ourselves of no reputation—to put our lives as we know and want them to death and to let God take over.

Why? The kingdom of heaven is ours. We have such greater riches than what are found here on earth, and even on earth, we can partake in great riches that the world is searching for—dying for: love, peace, joy, acceptance, truth, comfort...happiness.

What did the humility of Christ bring? Exaltation. Jesus was lifted up. "Wherefore God also hath highly exalted him, and given him a name which is above every name: That at the name of Jesus every knee should bow, of things in heaven, and things in earth, and things under the earth; And that every tongue should confess that Jesus Christ is Lord, to the glory of God the Father." (Philippians 2:9-11) Also, because of Christ's humility, salvation is available to all who will believe. "And no man hath ascended up to heaven, but he that came down from heaven, even the Son of man which is in heaven. And as Moses lifted up the serpent in the wilderness, even so must the Son of man be lifted up: That whosoever believeth in him should not perish, but have eternal life. For God so loved the world, that he gave his only begotten Son, that whosoever believeth in him should not perish, but have everlasting life. For God sent not his Son into the world to condemn the world; but that the world through him might be saved. He that believeth on him is not condemned: but he that believeth not is condemned already, because he hath not believed in the name of the only begotten Son of God." (John 3:13-18)

King Nebuchadnezzar, who reigned during the ministry of Daniel and is found in the Book of Daniel (Chapters 1-4)[2], is an example of a person who chose pride. Nebuchadnezzar was the king of Babylon when Babylon was one of the strongest, most feared nations in the world. He was a brutal military general and a brilliant architect, building statutes and other landmarks the world had not known.

Nebuchadnezzar had everything going for him except one thing: he did not know God. So, instead of using all of his gifts and power for good, he worshipped himself—was prideful—and hurt people who did not join in the worship.

Nebuchadnezzar had threatened to kill all the wise men, including Daniel and his friends because no one could interpret his dream. God gave Daniel a vision that was able to tell Nebuchadnezzar the dream, and Nebuchadnezzar praised the Lord for a moment.

Not too long afterward, the king built a great statue of himself and told everyone that they had to bow to it or be thrown into a fiery furnace. Of those on the scene of this celebration of the king was Hananiah, Mishael and Azariah, Daniel's friends. They refused to bow down and were thrown into that furnace, but they did not burn, and Nebuchadnezzar again praised God for a moment.

When Nebuchadnezzar had another dream that troubled him, he knew to go to Daniel, but Daniel hesitated to tell the king the dream as it was not good for the king. God showed King Nebuchadnezzar that he was great; however, he would not be great for long and would be as an animal.

A year after that dream and warning from God through Daniel (who is a great example of being poor in spirit as well), Nebuchadnezzar began to boast of his greatness: "The king spake, and said, Is not this great Babylon, that I have built for my house of the kingdom by the might of my power, and for the honor of my majesty?" (Daniel 4:30)

In the midst of his prideful speech, God spoke to him: "While the word was in the king's mouth, there fell a voice from heaven, saying, O king Nebuchadnezzar, to thee it is spoken; The kingdom is departed from thee. And they shall drive thee from men, and thy dwelling shall be with the beasts of the field: they shall make thee to eat grass as oxen, and seven times shall pass over thee, until though know that the Most High ruleth in the kingdom of men, and giveth it to whomsoever He will." (Daniel 4:31-32)

Within the hour Nebuchadnezzar was eating grass as the oxen do, just as God had said. "The same hour was the thing fulfilled upon Nebuchadnezzar: and he was driven from men, and did eat grass as oxen, and his body was wet with the dew of heaven, till his hairs were grown like eagle's feathers, and his nails like birds' claws." (Daniel 4:33)

Nebuchadnezzar himself wrote "For four years my kingdom in the city . . .gave me no joy. During this time, not one building of any importance did I issue to be built; the precious treasures of my kingdom I did not lay out . . . I did not sing praises to Merodach, my god, nor did I provide his sacrificial table with offerings, nor did I clean any of the waterways."[3] Since the Babylonians only counted two seasons, summer and winter, this would make up the timeline that God said—seven seasons or periods of time.

The Bible tells us "For whosoever exalteth himself shall be abased; and he that humbleth himself shall be exalted." (Luke 14:11) Nebuchadnezzar is an example of one who exalted himself. He was prideful. Yet, He was brought low—very low. Abase means behave in a way that belittles or degrades (someone). We see that in this account. However, the opposite is also true that if we will humble ourselves, we will be exalted. We can see that with Daniel in this same account. For all of the details, read Daniel chapters 1-4.

Attitude is a choice; therefore, happiness is a choice. We can choose the attitude of humility, where we have wisdom and under-standing that we need God, even if we have power, wealth, and good looks as Nebuchadnezzar had (though I'm not sure about the looks). We will still miss out on peace, love, acceptance, and true happiness if we choose to look to those things to get us through life.

~ I ~

PART III: PERSONAL EXAMPLE

I will never forget the day that God looked down on me and heard my broken heart and sent one of His children to reach out to me and start me on this path of being poor in spirit. It was not just a one-time thing, although I was poor in spirit that day.

I can't explain the hurt and desperation that I felt. I was sad, lonely, and felt like every person that I love would be better off without me. I was broken, but I didn't know why. I didn't understand why. My life was not terrible. I was not without people—in fact, I was surrounded by people—friends and family were at my house daily. I had six children that I treasured.

However, I knew and felt that something was missing. Something was not right. The truth is that I wanted to die, and ironically, that was where God wanted me. That was the place where He could finally get through to me. I had let go of my life.

It's ironic, but most of us, no matter where we are, will go to prayer when we are broken and helpless. We pray out to God, and that is what I did. I begged Him to change my way of thinking, to help me, to heal me, to give me a different perspective because I had children that needed me.

During my prayer, my phone rang. On the other side of the line, was Mrs. Judi Meyer, a teacher and minister of Metropolitan Baptist Church, inviting me to a ladies' fellowship. How could I say no? I was just begging God for His help, and I couldn't ignore that this might be it. And it was.

It was that initial brokenness—that humility and being at a point where I knew that I couldn't do life the same way any longer and be okay. I needed change, but I couldn't bring it about. I needed peace that I couldn't produce. I needed love, which hadn't been met. I needed purpose, which I couldn't find. And I have found all those things and so much more in my personal relationship with Jesus.

It wasn't the tears. I had had those many a days and night. It wasn't even the prayer. I had done that lots of times as well. It wasn't the invite to church, though the fellowship and knowledge that came from going to church was and is essential to my relationship with my Lord. It was my heart. It was the attitude of being poor in spirit. That was the start of happiness for me.

No, I don't have a perfect life. No, I am not without struggles and pain; however, I have an anchor. I have promises to hold onto. I have love that doesn't make sense. I have peace that passes all understanding. I have the kingdom of heaven to look forward to, but also, I have the kingdom of heaven right here with me that I carry every day in which is my hope—my everything.

~ 1 ~

PART IV: GO DEEPER

1. What does the word "blessed" mean? (Using a Bible dictionary such as the Webster's 1828 dictionary is a great tool to look up words to better understand a passage.)

----

2. What does it mean to be poor in spirit?
Poor–

In–

Spirit–

----

3. Read 1 Corinthians 1:25-29. "For ye see your calling, brethren, how that not many wise men after the flesh, not many mighty, not many noble, are called: 27But God hath chosen the foolish things of the world to confound the wise; and God hath chosen the weak things of the world to confound the things which are mighty; 28And base things of the world, and things which are despised, hath God chosen, yea, and things which are not, to bring to nought things

that are: 29That no flesh should glory in his presence. 30But of him are ye in Christ Jesus, who of God is made unto us wisdom, and righteousness, and sanctification, and redemption: 31That, according as it is written, He that glorieth, let him glory in the Lord." (1 Corinthians 1:25-31)

a) According to these verses, what kind of people is God NOT calling?

----

b) What kind of people is God calling?

----

c) What two reasons are given that God calls the latter kind of people?

----

4. Read Daniel Chapters 1 and 2 and answer the following questions:

a) What qualities were the king's servants to look for in the young captives that they brought back to Babylon? (see Daniel Chapter 1 verses 3-5)

----

b) Who was chosen, according to Daniel Chapter 1 verse 6?

----

c) Based on the qualities that were looked for in these young men, could they have been prideful? Would you have been prideful?

____

____

d) When King Nebuchadnezzar asked Daniel if he was able to make known the interpretation of his dream, what was Daniel's response? (see Daniel 2:27-30)

____

____

____

e) Compare Daniel's response in those previous verses (Daniel 2:27-30) with Nebuchadnezzar's response in Daniel 4:30.

____

____

____

____

f) From what you know to be true about Daniel and Nebuchadnezzar, can you see how the above verses (1 Corinthians 1:25-29) and Luke 14:11 are shown in the lives of these two great men? What are some insights that you have gained?

____

____

____

____

____

5. Have you ever found yourself poor in spirit? Describe an account below.

____

____

____

____

____

6. Have you believed in your heart that Jesus is the fulfillment of all that you need? Why not, if you haven't?

____

____

7. What do you trust in today for your love? Joy? Peace? Acceptance? Happiness?

a) Are those things working for you?

~ 2 ~

BLESSED ARE THEY THAT MOURN

"Blessed are they that mourn: for they shall be comforted."
(Matthew 5:4)

Part I: Insight

What does it mean to mourn? It means to cry, right? To be sad—express grief or sorrow. How strange is it that Jesus would tell us that if we would cry, be sorrowful or grieve, then we will be happy (blessed)!

We must understand that Jesus did mean what He said. However, He was not referring to the sadness that you might be thinking of. Jesus was not telling us that we should be sad about who we are or the circumstances in our lives and then we will be happy. Unfortunately, we have experienced sadness—grief over losing someone close to us, someone hurting us or even consequences from our own foolish behavior. We have experienced sadness, but that sadness did not bring about happiness. So, is Jesus wrong?

Of course, Jesus is not wrong. In fact, a rule of thumb, as you read the Bible and you start to question things, know this: God is right, and we need to grow and agree with Him!

So, what in the world is Jesus talking about? What kind of sorrow/sadness brings about happiness? It is a godly sorrow. The Bible gives us the definition in 2 Corinthians "For godly sorrow worketh repentance to salvation not to be repented of: but the sorrow of the world worketh death." (2 Corinthians 7:10)

The sorrow that we immediately think about is the worldly sorrow. We are sad because something has happened to us or to someone that we love, and it makes us grieve. However, this grieving doesn't make us happy. In fact, we generally feel terrible, though it is a natural way to deal with things and a process that is needed for cleansing as long as you can move on to the next steps of acceptance and moving forward. So, worldly sorry is not a terrible thing. God is not against worldly sorrow in this way. In fact, the Bible tells us that "Jesus wept." (John 11:35)

Godly sorrow is different. Godly sorrow deals with the source of the sorrow. What are you sorry for? Godly sorrow is a sadness over sin in our lives. It is a sorrow that says, 'I have wronged God. I have been unfaithful to Him.' This sorrow leads us to repentance or a turning away from our sin. This is the sorrow that brings about happiness, and even though it is hard—I mean, it is sorrow—we will be comforted. Looking ahead we will look at two Biblical examples, and I will share a personal testimony about these two sorrows so that you may understand more clearly.

It comes down to this. We all sin. We all have consequences of sin, whether we are believers or not. God calls this the law of sowing and reaping. The world may call it karma which is a different thing altogether. When it comes down to dealing with that reaping of what we sowed—when we have to deal with the consequences—what are we sorry about? Are we sorry about the consequences? Or are we sorry about how we got to the consequences? That is the difference between worldly sorrow and godly sorrow.

An example could be that you lied on a job application. You thought it wasn't a big deal. You worked at the job for three months and were looking at a promotion. In the meantime, your boss found out that you lied on the application and fired you. Now, it would be painful to lose that job. It would cause a lot of uncertainty and real sorrow, but if that is all you feel, you may likely go out and lie on the very next job application that you fill out, extending your chance to repeat those same consequences.

However, if you are grieved because of the loss of the job and realize that you should not have lied on that application, considering God in your thoughts, you will still have to deal with those consequences, but you won't have more pain because you will turn from the behavior that brought about the circumstances.

There is a principle in RU that says "God balances guilt with blame. Accept the blame and God will remove the guilt." Sometimes a lot of our sorrow is balled up in one word: guilt. We are guilty that we have done this or that. We feel guilty that we hurt someone. We feel guilty...fill in the blanks, but that is not the voice of God that wants guilt in our lives. It is the voice of our enemy.

God wants us to repent. To have a godly sorrow—not feel beat up and worthless. "There is therefore now no condemnation to them which are in Christ Jesus, who walk not after the flesh, but after the Spirit." (Romans 8:1)

Satan condemns. God convicts. What is the difference? Shame or restoration. Both condemnation and conviction have to do with proclaiming us guilty of sin. The difference is where these two lead us. Condemnation says that you can't get it right and that there is no need to try to do better. It leads us further into sin instead of away from it, and therefore further away from God instead of close to Him. Conviction says that you are loved, and you hurt the One who loves you. He wants to clean you up and help you get back on track. Come to Him, so He can restore you. This brings you to repentance which draws you closer to God and away from sin—

how it should be. Sadness that just feels bad or Sorrow that leads to happiness—repentance and freedom. Those are the choices.

Four ways to tell the difference between condemnation and conviction are:

1)	**Conviction is specific.** Condemnation is vague.

2)	**Conviction provides a way out.** Condemnation traps you.

3)	**Conviction addresses the sin.** Condemnation accuses the person.

4)	**Conviction brings hope.** Condemnation brings hopelessness.

"If we confess our sins, He is faithful and just to forgive us our sins, and to cleanse us from all unrighteousness." (1 John 1:9) God wants a real relationship as a loving Father who knows all but still wants to be there to clean us up. When we confess (agree with Him), He will forgive and make us feel better too. That is that comfort that comes from God, from having a godly sorrow. We mourn and we get comforted, but we also mourn BECAUSE we are comforted. It is that position in Christ that makes us cry about our sin—mourn over it—and therefore repent and move forward.

What are you feeling bad about today? Is it a godly sorrow or a worldly sorrow? "Blessed are they that mourn: for they shall be comforted." (Matthew 5:3)

~ 2 ~

PART II: BIBLICAL EXAMPLE

David, A Man After God's Own Heart: An Example of Godly Sorrow

First, Jesus tells us that we are blessed (happy) if we are poor in spirit—if we will see ourselves in need of a Savior, in need of help. When we realize that we do not have what we need most, that is the place God wants us to be.

Now, He is saying that if we would mourn (grieve/cry), we will be happy (blessed). Like I've said before, Jesus' ways are definitely not ways that we are accustomed to. They even seem crazy! However, who can know better than He who knows all and has created all?

A primary example of this that we see in scripture is with David. King David was a mighty man, even from his youth. God had anointed him to be king of Israel as just a young kid (1 Samuel 16). He defeated the giant Goliath, while the army of Israel and King Saul himself shook in their boots (1 Samuel 17). He ministered to the king when he was low (1 Samuel 16:17-23). He became a mighty warrior in the army killing tens of thousands of soldiers of the enemies of God (1 Samuel 18:7).

As David took the throne as king, he had every reason to be prideful and entitled and he was. Because of that, one small compromise led to great disaster in David's life. As he became comfortable in himself and prideful in who he was in life (the opposite of being poor in spirit), he took a day off from work. While at home, he drifted off to the roof during a time when people would bathe and caught a glimpse of his neighbor's wife, Bathsheba. He did not take his eyes off her, called for her, and laid with her, though both of them were married to other people.

David fell into sin rather quickly. First, he took his eyes off Jesus. He forgot that without God, he was nothing. He forgot that he wouldn't have been anointed to be king, defeated Goliath or had been so successful in war or made it through the insanity of Saul while he tried to kill David. No, he trusted in himself and became selfish.

"And it came to pass, after the year was expired, at the time when kings go forth to battle, that David sent Joab, and his servants with him, and all Israel; and they destroyed the children of Ammon, and besieged Rabbah. But David tarried still at Jerusalem. And it came to pass in an eveningtide, that David arose from off his bed, and walked upon the roof of the king's house: and from the roof he saw a woman washing herself; and the woman was very beautiful to look upon. And David sent and inquired after the woman. And one said, Is not this Bathsheba, the daughter of Eliam, the wife of Uriah the Hittite? And David sent messengers, and took her; and she came in unto him, and he lay with her; for she was purified from her uncleanness: and she returned unto her house." (2 Samuel 11:1-4)

David, just as quickly as he fell into sin, found out that when we give into temptation the consequences are inevitable, incalculable, and up to God. Bathsheba became pregnant, and David tried to cover up the sin by having her husband come home and lie with her to pretend that the baby was his, but Uriah was a good man that would only stand to protect his king, so David had Uriah killed in battle to cover his sin.

Remember, we are studying "Blessed are they that mourn: for they shall be comforted." (Matthew 5:4) David was still prideful and continued to judge the people and go on with his life, hoping to look like a good guy as he took Bathsheba as his wife after her husband died in war.

However, God won't allow us, especially His children, to stay in darkness. David had gotten so far in sin that he couldn't see, and God sent the prophet Nathan to pull those blinders off. (2 Samuel 12:1-7) It was in that moment when David was told that He was the man—He was the one who was guilty. David's eyes were open, and He became broken. He began to mourn over his sin.

That dark time could not be forgotten as David still had to reap what he had sown; however, he was changed at that point. He was no longer in darkness. He was comforted by the Lord. He was forgiven because he repented. He found God's grace, mercy, and unconditional love was right there, and after that moment with the prophet, David wrote the great psalm of repentance, Psalm 51. He went on to do great things and lead the people with mighty faith and strength—still not perfect—but forever David is known as a man after God's own heart (Acts 13:22).

God has shown us that we are not going to be perfect, but we shouldn't let that be an excuse to sin, either. We must keep our accounts with Him short, meaning we should be broken when we have sinned against God. That is what it means to mourn in the context of this scripture. It is not just sad or down on yourself; it is hurt about how you have done the Almighty God who sent His Son to die for you. This should cause us to turn away from that sin and turn into His loving arms the way that David did. This will cause us to be happy, and we will be comforted.

David could've continued in his sin and acted like he had no clue what Nathan the prophet was talking about, and, he, like Saul, would've had a different outcome in life and we would speak of his name differently.

God's plan will be accomplished. He wants to use you for something. He had a plan for David, but David could've let his self-ishness be the ruler of his life and not God. God has a plan for each of us, and we can let our selfishness be our ruler instead of God. He will just pick someone else for the job. Here's the thing, God is God. His will will be done, but will we be in a place where we can be used for His kingdom? He has given us free will to choose what we will do...will we choose Him or self/sin/Satan and the world?

"He that covereth his sins shall not prosper: but whoso confesseth and forsaketh them shall have mercy." (Proverbs 28:13) "Behold, happy is the man whom God correcteth: therefore despise not thou the chastening of the Almighty:" (Job 5:17)

~ 2 ~

PART II: BIBLICAL EXAMPLE

Judas Iscariot, Follower with No Heart: An Example of Worldy Sorrow

Not everyone takes the opportunity to be forgiven and comforted from the sin in their lives. Some choose worldly sorrow over godly sorrow. Judas Iscariot, when faced with sorrow for betraying the Lord Jesus Christ did not repent. He only felt sorry for himself. He hated the consequences of his behavior, but he did not turn to God for forgiveness.

Jesus appointed 12 disciples to be close to him, to learn from him as He taught, perform miracles, and spread the gospel during His three-year earthly ministry. Judas was one of those 12 disciples. He learned directly from Jesus. He had intimate conversations, watched Jesus heal people, and witnessed lives be changed. He even performed miracles himself. Yet, Judas didn't recognize who He learned from. "And many other signs truly did Jesus in the presence of his disciples, which are not written in this book:" (John 20:30)

Judas was the treasurer of the bunch. Although he is known as the traitor now, no one would've guessed that he was a traitor among the rest of the disciples. When Jesus mentioned that one of the twelve would betray him, they all questioned whether it was themselves but didn't automatically point to Judas. No one could tell that he didn't believe in Jesus. "When Jesus had thus said, he was troubled in spirit, and testified, and said, Verily, verily, I say unto you, that one of you shall betray me. Then the disciples looked one on another, doubting of whom He spake. Now there was leaning on Jesus' bosom one of His disciples, whom Jesus loved. Simon Peter therefore beckoned to him, that he should ask who it should be of whom He spake. He then lying on Jesus' breast saith unto him, Lord, who is it? Jesus answered, He it is, to whom I shall give a sop, when I have dipped it. And when he had dipped the sop, He gave it to Judas Iscariot, the son of Simon. And after the sop Satan entered into him. Then said Jesus unto him, That thou doest, do quickly. Now no man at the table knew for what intent He spake this unto him." (John 13:21-28) It is undeniably sad when we think about Judas Iscariot and the opportunity that he was given and had even in the end.

Judas felt sorrow once he watched Jesus taken away in the middle of the night and dragged by those who wanted Him dead. He hurled the money that he was awarded for the betrayal—30 pieces of silver—toward those leaders who would not accept it. However, his heart didn't turn to God. Instead, Judas went within, had personal sorrow, and hung himself. How sad!

"Then Judas, which had betrayed him, when he saw that he was condemned, repented himself, and brought again the thirty pieces of silver to the chief priests and elders, Saying, I have sinned in that I have betrayed the innocent blood. And they said, What is that to us? see thou to that. And he cast down the pieces of silver in the temple, and departed, and went and hanged himself." (Matthew 27:3-5)

It is natural to have worldly sorrow, but that worldly sorrow should open our eyes to something deeper—that godly sorrow that God hopes we will all come to know. Judas had the worldly sorrow—he recognized that he did wrong, but he missed the step of repentance. True repentance. How do we know? Because he killed himself. Had he turned to God, he would've been forgiven—

comforted—just as the Scriptures tell us. We will either have self-ishness or salvation. "Blessed are they that mourn: for they shall be comforted." (Matthew 5:4)

~ 2 ~

PART III: PERSONAL EXAMPLE

For many years, I had no clue there were different sorrows. I only knew worldly sorrow. In fact, when I first repented to the Lord, turning from the way life had always been toward Him, I was in worldly sorrow. It was my worldly sorrow that turned me to Him.

Day after day I felt sorry for myself. I felt alone. I didn't feel as if I mattered to anyone—that everyone would be better off without me. I battled thoughts of suicide daily. I mourned my situation. I mourned my relationships. I mourned my feelings, but that didn't bring about change.

It did, however, bring me to my God whom I had put in the back of my mind for a decade. I remember that day— January 30th, 2013. It was a Wednesday. The kids were at school and Patrick was at work. I felt such a deep sadness that it hurt. My tears stung as they came down my face, and in the midst of that pain, I cried out to God in my living room.

I begged God to hear me and to take away those feelings of unhappiness. I had so much to be happy for. I loved my children, and I talked to my Heavenly Father about how I didn't understand why I felt the way I did; I just wanted change. Everything felt hopeless. I was pregnant and Patrick and I were splitting up.

As I cried out that Wednesday morning or possibly afternoon, my phone rang. Right in the middle of my deep prayer, the phone rang. Usually, I would ignore the phone in times such as that, but something told me to answer it. It was like I knew that it was God wanting me to answer, and so I did.

On the other end of that line was Mrs. Judi Meyer. To me, she was just a nice lady from church who often wrote cards to the girls. That day she invited me to church—Ladies Fellowship that would happen the next day.

I couldn't deny that indeed it was God that had sent Mrs. Judi to call that day. Especially as I look back, I have no doubt that it was a divine intervention, and I am so thankful that Judi Meyer was in a position to hear God that day because I needed Him. My kids needed Him. My children's father needed Him.

Again, I was mourning over my life and how I felt about it and I called out to God. When I went to church, I started reading the Bible for the first time, really. We were in the Book of Esther. I'll never forget it. I went to the next church service that Sunday. It was unorthodox, but I felt welcomed and went to the next service after that.

There, my life truly changed. God talked to me directly as I sat on that chair in the church service. He showed me who He is and who I am. I wept over my sin and committed my heart and my life to Him that day, and, praise God, He has not let me go. He has not given up on me. He has held onto me, and I have found the greatest purpose and true happiness that cannot be taken away because it has nothing to do with my circumstances.

"Blessed are they that mourn: for they shall be comforted." (Matthew 5:4) It may have been a mourning for my situation that first brought me to God, but it was a mourning over my sin that brought me to repentance and enabled me to give my whole heart to God.

How would you explain your mourning? Are you sad over where you are in life or what someone has done to you? God will hear you and heal you if you go to Him. "For whosoever shall call upon the name of the Lord shall be saved." (Romans 10:13) However, we must believe that God is God and that He can save before we will ever call out to Him. "But without faith it is impossible to please Him: for he that cometh to God must believe that He is, and that He is a rewarder of them that diligently seek Him." (Hebrews 11:6)

You see, I didn't know much about God when I cried out to Him that winter day in 2013, but I had just enough faith that He was there, that He is God, and that He could do something about where I was.

Do you believe that? Have you called out to Him?

It wasn't until after I gave Him my heart that I got to know more and more about Him, and I only love Him more. I became more dedicated to God as I got to know His heart and amazing love He has for us. I say this because it is faith that will bring us to a place where we even want to get knowledge. Faith, according to scripture, is looking to something that we can't see, hoping in that Person. "Now faith is the substance of things hoped for, the evidence of things not seen." (Hebrews 11:1)

My daughter goes on these Instagram live feeds, and she hopes that one of these celebrities will choose her to do a live chat with. She has faith that one day she will be picked. Well, just a couple of weeks ago, she was picked. One of the celebrities from one of her favorite shows chose her to do a live chat, and there she was in front of thousands of other fans talking with this actress. She was so excited. She still talks about it with the same excitement today.

That's pretty amazing. However, do we sometimes think that God is too high that we can't reach Him? Sure, there are lots of people who don't try to go on those live feeds because they figure they'll never get to talk to that celebrity. And, no doubt, many people don't call out to God because they think that He is too high to reach.

What's even more amazing is that although God is way higher than any celebrity on earth, He is not too high for us. He, in fact, wants to spend time with us—each of us—individually every single day. He wants to have a relationship with us, and He sent His only begotten Son to die for our sins so that it was possible. Jesus came to earth and felt temptation and experienced loss and pain so that He can understand us more. "For we have not an high priest which cannot be touched with the feeling of our infirmities; but was in all points tempted like as we are, yet without sin." (Hebrews 4:15)

We don't have to wait in line and hope that He will pick us. All we have to do is call out to Him in faith and He will hear us. No matter what we are mourning for at the first, He will bring us to a place where we can see clearly who He is which will make ourselves be transparent, and we will see our sin in light of the blood of Christ, shed because of my sin—our sins—and then we can mourn over sin.

Once we mourn over our sin, we will be comforted. To experience the comfort that God gives brings joy—a level of happiness that isn't changed by outside pressures or situations.

Eight years ago, I was in a place of mourning, but God reached down into my soul and began to transform me, little by little, and though I still struggle when I get my eyes off of Him, thinking that my situations are supposed to make me happy, it isn't long that I'm brought back to the foot of the cross and I can see my sins upon the back of the innocent Savior. And I see an unmatched love. There my thoughts are changed from sadness to gladness of just how blessed I truly am.

~ 2 ~

PART IV: GO DEEPER

1. What is the difference between worldly sorrow and godly sorrow?

----

2. Is worldly sorrow a sin? Why or why not?

----

3. Consider a time in your life when you had worldly sorrow. What was the outcome (restored/lost friendship, item, respect...etc.)?

----

4. Considering that same time, how might it have been different if you had a godly sorrow over that same instance?

---

5. Can you think of a time when you truly experienced a godly sorrow? Write about it below. How did God comfort you?

---

6. Consider King Saul in 1 Samuel 15. In verse 24, he says that he has sinned. Do you think that Saul has a worldly sorrow or a godly sorrow? What evidence do you see in this Chapter that supports that?

---

7. Consider Peter in Matthew 26:75 and Acts 2:36-38. Do you think Peter had a worldly sorrow or a godly sorrow? What evidence do you see that supports that?

---

8. Knowing the difference of the two sorrows, what do you intend to do differently as you deal with grief and sin?

~ 3 ~

BLESSED ARE THE MEEK

"Blessed are the meek: for they shall inherit the earth." (Matthew 5:5)

Part I—Insight: Gaining Knowledge

In society today, you will not hear the word meek. It is a word that is shunned by the world that we live in, particularly in America. To be meek is to be mild of temper, soft, gentle, not easily provoked. Even deeper, it means that when there is friction, one eases the tension. According to RU, the definition for meekness is "the ability for God's people to negotiate among others without causing friction."

I believe most people would call meek "weak." You might think, how can I be happy if I let people walk all over me, but meekness is not weakness. It is great strength, in fact. Meekness comes from our state of mind—a higher thinking. One who is meek knows that they inherit the earth, and they don't need to fight every battle with every person that they encounter. These things are trivial. They have set their hearts on things above. "But the meek shall inherit the earth; and shall delight themselves in the abundance of peace." (Psalm 37:11)

Jesus understands the great value of meekness. See, we live in a fallen world where we all are prone to sin. We are prone to character weaknesses and living by our feelings. It is a person that is meek that can get us to reconciliation—peace.

Happiness will not come by us recognizing our feelings and living for them, no matter how many times the world tells us to follow our hearts. It is a terrible strategy. Why? Because our hearts are deceitful above all things and desperately wicked, the Bible tells us in Jeremiah 17:9. So, as one who is trying to be happy, how can it make sense that I take steps after deceit and wickedness? Yet, that it is what my heart is. Ecclesiastes warns us that "He that loveth silver shall not be satisfied with silver; nor he that loveth abundance with increase: this is also vanity." (Ecclesiastes 5:10)

Therefore, we are instructed in the bible to guard our hearts: "Keep thy heart with all diligence; for out of it are the issues of life." (Proverbs 4:23) This is saying protect your heart. That is what the word "keep" means. It is an old English military word to watch and stand guard. Why should we protect our hearts? Because everything that we do comes from the heart.

Let me make clear that the heart in the Bible is not talking about the actual heart that pumps blood in our bodies. It is the seat of our emotions and interchangeable with the word soul. It is our thoughts, feelings, and desires.

Therefore, by that definition, you can surely see that everything comes from our hearts. Every thought affects our feelings, actions, and desires. It is in our thoughts, in fact, that spiritual warfare begins therefore we must teach our hearts and guard them by being in the Bible and allowing God to transform our minds.

Meekness is not just something that happens. It is a fruit of the Spirit or an outcome of yielding to the Spirit of God. See, if we are saved, we have two natures—the old, sinful nature that is selfish and likes to follow the heart and the new nature which is born of God and desires righteousness and building up the kingdom of God. "That ye put off concerning the former conversation the old man, which is corrupt according to the deceitful lusts; And be renewed in the spirit of your mind; And that ye put on the new man, which after God is created in righteousness and true holiness." (Ephesians 4:22-24) These two natures are in constant battle every day.

All of the beatitudes (Be Attitudes) are yielding to God's way—the new nature—and rejecting the old way that comes natural to us. Again, it is not an automatic thing, and without the Spirit of God it is impossible. However, with God all things are possible. "But Jesus beheld them, and said unto them, With men this is impossible; but with God all things are possible." (Matthew 19:26)

Meekness, specifically, is saying I know there is a problem, but I am not going to make it worse. Instead, I am going to rely on my God and find something good in this thing. There are two people in the Bible who are defined as being meek, Moses and Jesus. We will discuss their character further along in this chapter. However, considering them, we can see strong leadership that overcame struggles, rebellion, and flat-out rejection. Yet, they still made a difference in many lives and still are making a difference today. It was that meekness that provided the way to influence. And who doesn't want to influence the world around them?

This is part of God's plan. There is a world that is against itself—many people who are choosing to live for themselves and don't care who gets hurt as an expense. They follow their deceitful, wicked hearts and are blind to the truth. God's people are to be meek. We are to be able to deal with those kinds of people with kindness and compassion, helping them to see the truth. "And the servant of the Lord must not strive; but be gentle unto all men, apt to teach, patient, in meekness instructing those that oppose themselves; if God peradventure will give them repentance to the acknowledging of the truth." (2 Timothy 2:23-24) Why? So, that they too may be restored and have salvation. "For the LORD taketh pleasure in His people: He will beautify the meek with salvation." (Psalm 149:4)

How does meekness bring happiness? You may still be asking that question. Well, God made us on purpose and for a purpose. Fulfilling the purpose of God brings joy within our hearts. It is hard to explain, but it is available for anyone who will walk with Him. "The meek also shall increase their joy in the LORD,..." (Isaiah 29:19)

This is an attitude—a choice and an understanding. It is a position in Christ. Notice these are called BE Attitudes. To be means exist or to happen. These are attitudes that exist or happen in our lives which bring happiness.

So, it is not a to-do checklist that brings happiness. I told you that this is not one of those books. I am showing what Jesus taught is the way to happiness—change your mind to KNOW your position. Let meekness exist in your life BECAUSE you have inherited the earth. You don't have to worry about the small arguments in this world. We who are saved inherit all that Jesus has inherited. This life is temporary. "The Spirit itself beareth witness with our spirit, that we are the children of God: And if children, then heirs; heirs of God, and joint-heirs with Christ; if so be that we suffer with him, that we may be also glorified together. (Romans 8:16-17)

~ 3 ~

PART II: BIBLICAL EXAMPLE

Moses, A Man of Meekness

Moses was a man of meekness. The Bible says "(Now the man Moses was very meek, above all the men which were upon the face of the earth.)" (Numbers 12:3) Remember meekness is shown when there is already conflict, and Moses led the Israelites during a time when they were very "stiff-necked," according to the Word of God.

In this verse where Moses is mentioned to be very meek (more than any other that was upon the earth), we can see that friction is in abundance. Not just friction—but family friction. Numbers Chapter 12 gives us an interesting account that highlights the meekness of Moses and is a great example for us to understand what meekness truly is.

This chapter starts with people speaking against Moses. This was a regular occurrence to Moses from the time that he led in freeing the Israelites from slavery in the land of Egypt. However, on that particular day, it was his older brother and sister that led the attack against him.

The Bible says "And Miriam and Aaron spake against Moses because of the Ethiopian woman whom he had married: for he had married an Ethiopian woman. And they said, Hath the LORD indeed spoken only by Moses? Hath He not spoken also by us? And the LORD heard it." (Numbers 12:1-2)

Notice the indication of prejudice and nationalism (what some will call racism) occurring here. Miriam and Aaron had no other occasion against Moses except that his wife was from another nation. She was African (a Cushite). They were basically saying that the people shouldn't listen to him any longer—that God can speak through them as well.

Notice the silence of Moses. He could've responded in discord as his siblings spoke against his wife and challenged his leadership...in front of the whole congregation!

Most of all, notice the compassion of our Lord. "And the LORD heard it."

Moses' meekness comes from knowing who God is. Was he hurt? No doubt! Was he angry? Possibly. But he didn't rely on his feelings in that moment. He didn't give into his flesh (old nature), but he relied on the Spirit of God and displayed the fruit of the Spirit, meekness. (Remember the RU definition of meekness–the ability of God's people to negotiate among others without causing friction.)

Not only did Moses show meekness by remaining silent in that moment of betrayal, but as you read on in this passage, he goes even further in showing the Spirit of God in his life toward his siblings.

God called all three of them out of the congregation. He pulled Miriam and Aaron aside and basically said, 'I called Moses to be a prophet, why aren't you afraid to speak out against him?' And before the eyes of Aaron and Moses, as the cloud departed (the cloud symbolizing God Himself), Miriam became leprous. (Numbers 12:4-10)

Aaron looked to Moses and apologized. He admitted their sin and recognized that Moses had influence with God. He said, "Let her (Miriam) not be as one dead..." to his younger brother, Moses. (Numbers 12:12)

Moses didn't have an in with God because he was some great and mighty man who did everything right all the time. Moses could go to God and expect God to hear him and work according to His will because Moses believed God, respected God, and obeyed God. That is faith!

Moses had faith and instead of holding a grudge and letting his siblings suffer a little bit as one of us might be prone to do, he cried out to God to heal her in that very moment. The Bible says that he begged God. "And Moses cried unto the LORD, saying, Heal her now, O God, I beseech thee." (Numbers 12:13)

What a great example of meekness! Moses had a strong confidence in who his God was, and he waited for God to handle the friction. For us to have meekness, we must know God. God had proved himself to Moses from situation after situation of responding to evil people (such as Pharaoh and Korah) and rebellious people (as in the children of Israel who had to wander for 40 years because of their rebellion).

In case you think that meekness is only sitting back quietly and showing strength as you wait on God (though that can be meekness), it is also courageously facing danger to stand up for what is right as we can see with Moses as he faced the most powerful man on the earth during the time of the exodus and told him to let go the people whom he was holding as slaves—God's people, the Hebrews. Confidently Moses was a vessel as God poured out wrath upon Pharaoh and the Egyptian people. Again, meekness is not weakness. It is strength with control.

When we get to know God, it is unfortunate that not everyone will take kindly to the changes that God brings to our lives. Instead of dealing with the light that God tries to show others through us, people reject that light (ultimately rejecting God), but it will manifest in a rejection of us in the moment. Sometimes people just have bad days. Other times we have to deal with people that openly hate God and anyone who will stand with Him. These are things we will have to face as Christians, but God made provision for us. He didn't just send us out to the wolves to be eaten up! He gave us the Spirit of God!

So, we see the outcome of one who walks in meekness—one who is led by the Spirit of God. Moses was a great leader who was still influencing people at the time of Jesus and even now we are positively impacted by the life that Moses led. He made a difference for God. Moses was not a perfect man (which when you begin to study the Bible, you will realize that no man or woman that God used was perfect). However, because of Moses' reliance on God, salvation came to many. He shows us that happiness is found in following God.

Moses had opportunity to be raised up as a king in Pharoah's family in the land of Egypt. He had an opportunity to skip all the need for meekness in his life. He could've trusted circumstances to bring him happiness. However, He chose God and God's calling. "By faith Moses, when he was come to years, refused to be called the son of Pharaoh's daughter; Choosing rather to suffer affliction with the people of God, than to enjoy the pleasures of sin for a season; Esteeming the reproach of Christ greater riches than the treasures in Egypt: for he had respect unto the recompence of the reward." (Hebrews 11:24-26)

$$\sim 3 \sim$$

PART II: BIBLICAL EXAMPLE

Jesus, Meek but not Weak

Another example of meekness is given by Jesus. It is a description of Himself that He gives. "Take my yoke upon you, and learn of me; for I am meek and lowly in heart: and ye shall find rest unto your souls." (Matthew 11:29)

I believe that the worst portrayal of Jesus is that of some weak and feeble man. He says, "I am meek and lowly in heart." It is obvious that people have perceived this as weak and feeble. The reality is that Jesus was anything but weak.

As Jesus walked the earth, He displayed a strong confidence in the Father. A confidence that prevented him from giving into earthly temptations but remaining strong and sinless throughout His life on earth.

Jesus was not without friction in His life as He walked the earth. The people that He came for rejected Him, despised Him, and killed Him. He knew this would happen, yet He had compassion on the lost, the weak, and the sick. He healed those who would believe. He preached to all and warned of judgment for those who would not repent. He went against the grain of the day, which was religion and good works. He taught about relationship and a heart attitude—the motive behind things being more important than the act itself. And the leaders did not like it!

The Bible gives us a clear picture of what meekness is in Jesus. "Let nothing be done through strife or vainglory; but in lowliness of mind let each esteem other better than themselves. Look not every man on his own things, but every man also on the things of others. Let this mind be in you, which was also in Christ Jesus: Who, being in the form of God, thought it not robbery to be equal with God: But made himself of no reputation, and took upon Him the form of a servant, and was made in the likeness of men: And being found in fashion as a man, He humbled himself, and became obedient unto death, even the death of the cross." (Philippians 2:3-8)

Jesus had the power to think a person out of existence. He could snap His fingers and make a person have leprosy. He had legions of angels at His command. Yet, as He dealt with jealous and power-hungry leaders who wanted to trick Him, take away His influence, and eventually murder Him, Jesus always responded with mercy and grace. Even though He knew their end was hell, He warned them of it. He gave them opportunity to repent.

I can think of no better example of meekness than when Jesus was taken in the middle of the night and falsely accused of blasphemy. Jesus prayed in agony that if there be another way to save the world that God would take the cup of wrath that was to come. He humbled Himself there, surrendering His will to that of the Father, and when one of His disciples, Judas Iscariot, came to give Him the kiss of betrayal, He called Him "friend."

The soldiers came in with swords to take Him away, but Jesus surrendered to them and even rebuked Peter for cutting off one of the soldier's ears, while then healing that soldier's same ear. He didn't speak as they brought Him up and falsely accused Him over and over again. He kept quiet as they whipped Him with the flagellum (also known as the cat-o-nine tails). Even as they punched Him in the face, pulled His beard, and tore His clothes, He said not a word. (This account is found in Matthew 26–27, Mark 15–16, Luke 22–23, and in John 18–19)

He only spoke a few times. One time He spoke to one of the thieves on the cross, the one who knew he was a sinner and seen that Jesus was the Savior. Jesus told that man that He would see him in paradise. (Luke 23:39-43) Also, before He gave up the ghost, He prayed that God the Father would forgive those who were murdering Him.

Compassion, love, and forgiveness down to His last breath before He would take on that punishment of death that we all owe. Meekness is not weakness. Strength is exhibited in Jesus' life and in the life of Moses and before you think that meekness is letting bad things happen to you and just lying down and taking it, Moses and Jesus had to confront people many times. They were not just pushovers; however, they weren't bullies either. They had a purpose when they confronted people and it was never to stick up for themselves. It was to stick up for God!

~ 3 ~

PART III: PERSONAL EXAMPLE

Meekness is one of those qualities that I would've thought was weakness eight years ago before I surrendered to Christ, and even up to three years after. It is a hard saying to "Let nothing be done through strife or vainglory; but in lowliness of mind let each esteem other better than themselves. Look not every man on his own things, but every man also on the things of others. Let this mind be in you, which was also in Christ Jesus:" (Philippians 2:3-4)

We just aren't raised to have this kind of mindset anymore, unless one is raised in a Christian home. I was raised with principles of standing up for your family, fighting for yourself and others, and hurting people before they ever get the chance to hurt you.

Day after day I witnessed the women in my family with black eyes and busted lips because of the men in their lives. My home as a child was full of terror-filled nights as I would hear banging and throwing and yelling, and I could do nothing about it. I would cry all night long and try to cover my head with my pillow and it always hurt me to see my mom the next morning.

Something within me said that would never be me! Unfortunately, that same mindset influenced my relationships when I started dating. Instead of ever getting hit by a man, when I felt hurt or mistreated or a man's voice got raised, I would hit him. I had become the monsters that hurt the women in my family as I was growing up.

Because of my pride, anger, and hurt, I thought it was okay (in the moment) to lash out. I don't know if I thought it was helping me get my way. I do know, however, that I never felt good about it afterward, but it was a problem of mine. A serious problem. I would continuously return to that kind of behavior.

At the age of 20, I was finally arrested for my violent behavior. I wish I could say that I learned my lesson and changed, but I had not. That violence still roared within me and though that toxic relationship of my youth was over, I had begun a new relationship and brought the same baggage with me.

A decade into that relationship and I was still a monster with violence and rage when I felt hurt or betrayed and even though I felt bad about it every time afterwards, I could not fix myself from this anger. I had six children by that time. Sadly, I did not protect them from hearing those same terror-filled noises that I despised as a child.

Finally, in January 2013, God brought me to the end of myself. I could not deal with those outbursts of violence anymore. I didn't want to feel lonely and angry any longer. In fact, at that time, as I mentioned before, I was wanting to die. I thought everyone was better off without me.

When I prayed there in my living room that cold, Wednesday afternoon and my phone rang, I knew I had to answer and I am so thankful that I did! I was finally in a position of being poor in spirit. I realized that I couldn't do this life alone anymore. I needed help. I was broken over the person that I had become. I wanted to be more—for my kids particularly.

A week and a half later, after attending Ladies Fellowship and the second worship service, I gave my life to God. I completely surrendered. I wanted what He had for me.

As I started attending those services every week and reading my Bible, it became clear to me that following God was different than I had ever imagined. I became a disciple of Jesus through the RU program which kept me in my Bible every day and challenged me to think about the things I was learning and put them to use in my life.

Still, I had not heard of meekness yet, and my then-boyfriend and I were always arguing. Anger was still a stronghold for me. Unfortunately, instead of showing meekness, that fruit of the Spirit of God working in me, I was showing discord. RU defines discord as "any disagreement which produces angry passions, contest, disputes, litigation or war." It is from a yielding to our old nature—the opposite of meekness.

I'm not sure when it started happening, but God changed the way I reacted to things at some point. It wasn't a conscious thing (except for the fact that I had been studying and meditating on His Word consistently). I didn't necessarily TRY to stop yelling, screaming, cussing, and hitting.

One day I felt extremely attacked by my then-boyfriend and I remember my response was not yelling and hitting. I didn't even realize it at first. I walked away from him and prayed and that is when I realized that I was actually filled with the Spirit in that moment. That stuff that I was learning about in RU about Jesus and the Word of God was actually happening in my life! Wow!

I cannot say that I never had an outburst of anger again. That would be a lie. However, I can say that it has been at least seven years since I put my hands on my husband and I testify that it is not me that is able to display such meekness, but it is indeed a fruit (outcome) of the Spirit of God working in me.

There will be no greater test to apply meekness than that with our closest friends and family. They are the ones we feel the most comfortable with and are more capable of letting our guards down. Being a wife and a mother have serious challenges...daily. There is always friction that needs not be accelerated. Surely, many of you know what I am talking about.

I am a homeschool mom. I school all of my children at home with help from my oldest daughter who assists with my youngest daughter's teaching. I have found this position to be very challenging, especially when it comes to teaching math.

Recently, during a math class, one of my children was having a hard time. She was starting to give up. I was also doing work because I work from home, and every time I would try to pause from work and help her, she would start breaking down and refused to hear what I was saying. So, I would go back to my work (still in the same room). Then she would start to say how I was no help, and another child joined in, and it got super hostile very quickly.

Generally, this would be a point of break down for me. I would need to escape to the bathroom for several minutes and cry and pray and hope that I can get composure to return to class and work. That day, I said a small prayer "Lord, help me" and God began to give me grace and that is what poured from me.

I didn't get overwhelmed. I rebuked my kids for being disrespectful. I gave my struggling child time to calm down, and I continued working as they finished their assignment. I then worked with that child later in the day on that assignment, and you know what, it wasn't the end of the world.

As I rebuked the children and got back to my job, I felt relief and pride (not in myself because I knew that I didn't do that). I thought of meekness. I thought of the Holy Spirit's present help at that very moment when I needed Him. Now, that moment is something that I can hold onto and remember that God was there, and He will be again. When we are reliant on Him, He shows up.

I, unfortunately, fail in meekness too often. It is way too easy to rely on myself than on God, and when I do, I handle the rough situations poorly. That is when God wants to show up and be the light in the situation—when times are rough or a situation is tough—even in the simple example of one day at school.

I feel like sometimes we only think of God in big things. We only seek Him in the large things, but God cares about the little things as well. In fact, the Bible tells us that if we would be faithful in the small things, we will be faithful in the big things: "He that is faithful in that which is least is faithful also in much: and he that is unjust in the least is unjust also in much." (Luke 16:10)

"The ceaseless chagrin of a self-centered life can be removed at once by learning Meekness and Lowliness of heart. He who learns them is forever proof against it. He lives henceforth a charmed life."

— Henry Drummond

"Meekness is the right us of power, and wisdom is the right use of knowledge. They go together. The truly wise person will show in his daily life that he is a child of God. Attitude and action go together. — Warren Wiersbe

~ 3 ~

PART IV: GO DEEPER

1. What is the definition of meekness?

____

____

____

2. Has this seemed like a weakness to you? Why or why not?

____

____

____

____

____

3. Considering 2 Timothy 2:24-26, answer the following questions:

"And the servant of the Lord must not strive; but be gentle unto all men, apt to teach, patient, In meekness instructing those that oppose themselves; if God peradventure will give them repentance to the acknowledging of the truth; And that they may recover themselves out of the snare of the devil, who are taken captive by him at his will." (2 Timothy 2:24-26)

a) According to these verses, are Christians supposed to argue and fight (strive) with other people?

____

____

----

b) What four qualities should the person of God have, according to these verses?

----

c) Who should the Christian instruct, according to these verses?

----

d) What are the two "r's" God might give to that one if we will do our part and show His love to them?

----

4. Review the verses and answers above. Why do you think that God finds it important that we show meekness?

----

5. Is meekness something that we will naturally respond with?

----

6. The Word of God and prayer need to be priorities if we are going to yield to the Spirit of God, which will give us the ability to respond in meekness.

a) How much time do you spend in the Word every day?

----

b) Every week?

----

c) How much time do you spend in prayer every day? (take some time to evaluate those questions HONESTLY and then add five minutes to that this week, so if you don't read your Bible at all, read it for five minutes a day. The same goes for prayer.) Buy a journal/ notebook and write about these things.

~ 4 ~

BLESSED ARE THOSE WHICH DO HUNGER AND THIRST AFTER RIGHTEOUSNESS

"Blessed are they which do hunger and thirst after righteousness: for they shall be filled." (Matthew 5:6)

Part I—Insight: Gaining Knowledge

A lot of times our happiness or lack of happiness comes from what we are filled with. This verse indicates an importance of desire. Again, blessed means divinely favored or supremely happy. That is our goal—to be supremely happy. "Hunger and thirst" here means to pine, to famish, or to crave (desire). Righteousness is to be right in the eyes of God; purity of heart; the perfection or holiness of His nature; and/or faithfulness, and to be filled means satisfied; made full and/or supplied with abundance.

If we paraphrase this verse, we might say 'happy are those who have a desire to be right before God because they shall be supplied with abundance.' The key word there is desire. That is what hunger and thirst is. As humans, hunger and thirst are some things that we can certainly relate to. We wake up and are usually hungry and thirsty. That hunger or thirst compels us to get something to eat or drink. It is a driving force of our actions.

Hunger and thirst can often be toward a particular object, not just general hunger or thirst. For instance, when I wake up in the morning, I am not thirsty for orange juice, milk, or water. I have a thirst for coffee first thing in the morning. It is a particular drink.

When it comes to other appetites of life—what entertains us or makes us happy—we too have unique appetites. However, just like that appetite for a particular drink can change, so can the appetite of entertainment or joy.

God made us to have a particular hunger and thirst after Him. Therefore, we are often not satisfied. It has always been the desire of God to have a relationship with mankind. When Adam and Eve disobeyed in the Garden of Eden and sin entered the world, God began to execute the plan of His only begotten Son dying on the cross for the sins of the world so that we can enjoy in that relationship again. "For God so loved the world, that he gave his only begotten Son, that whosoever believeth in him should not perish, but have everlasting life. For God sent not his Son into the world to condemn the world; but that the world through him might be saved." (John 3:16-17)

In the meantime, He gave us pictures of what that looks like—what salvation looks like. In Genesis Chapter three, everything was perfect. Adam and Eve had a perfect life with a perfect relationship with God. Their hunger and thirst were filled by all of the trees of the garden (except one). Their entertainment and happiness were fulfilled in God, each other, and the beautiful creation around them that they enjoyed. How do I know that? At the end of Genesis 1, the Bible says: "And God saw every thing that He had made, and behold, it was very good." (Genesis 1:31a)

To prevent confusion, Chapter two is a focused account of the creation of mankind particularly. It takes part of Chapter one and zooms in to the particulars of the creation of Adam and Eve. So, the end of Chapter one is still referring to this account in Chapter two—that everything was very good.

That perfect life that the first couple experienced was shaken when Satan came on the scene in Chapter three. It isn't known how long Adam and Eve enjoyed perfection, but I would guarantee that they regretted the decision to look for satisfaction elsewhere once they ate of that forbidden fruit.

Eve ate and gave to her husband. The Bible says, "And the eyes of them both were opened, and they knew that they were naked; and they sowed fig leaves together, and made themselves aprons." (Genesis 3:7) Immediately, they felt shame and tried to cover themselves.

Peace, comfort, and happiness were out the window! They then knew guilt, shame, regret, and a fear that they hadn't known before. So, when God called out to Adam, they "hid" from His presence. Of course, we know there is no hiding from the presence of God, but we still try to do it sometimes today, don't we?

They started playing the blame game when God confronted them. Eve blamed the serpent (aka Satan), Adam blamed Eve and God. They went from perfection to disaster in just one moment. Why? Because they had an appetite that wasn't of God. They weren't satisfied with the filling that they had.

Yet, God still showed His mercy by taking off their covering and sacrificing an innocent animal in their stead. That is the greatest picture of salvation that the Jewish people would continue to partake in year after year for the atonement of sin—an innocent dying for the guilty. Of course, that was a picture of Jesus, the perfect Lamb, that would come and die for the sins of the world and conquer sin and death by raising from the dead. "For Christ also hath once suffered for sins, the just for the unjust, that he might bring us to God, being put to death in the flesh, but quickened by the Spirit:" (1 Peter 3:18)

God gave His Word in the ten commandments (the Law) that brought people to the realization that they were sinners and needed forgiveness. We still have His Word today which should accomplish that same goal to point us to Jesus.

Ever since that moment, mankind has tried to fill that God-sized hole in our lives with so many things, from the act of religion to a love of money or even drugs and alcohol. We know something is missing. Yet, we are never satisfied. Solomon wrote in Ecclesiastes, "...the eye is not satisfied with seeing, nor the ear filled with hearing...neither is the eye satisfied with riches...he that loveth silver shall not be satisfied with silver; nor he that loveth abundance with increase: this is also vanity." (Ecclesiastes 1:8, 3:8 and 5:10) These words came from a man that had it all! No one has ever been wealthier than Solomon, and no man wiser either, except Jesus. He had everything that he could desire, yet he concluded that it was vanity—it didn't satisfy. In fact, he wrote: "Let us hear the conclusion of the whole matter: Fear God, and keep his commandments: for this is the whole duty of man." (Ecclesiastes 12:13)

His conclusion is similar to what Jesus is saying in this Beatitude: "Blessed are they which do hunger and thirst after righteousness, for they shall be filled." (Matthew 5:6)

So, what does it mean to hunger and thirst after righteousness and how can it be obtained? First, we must understand that righteousness means to be right in the eyes of God. We cannot do this alone. No matter if we dedicated our entire lives to good and giving to charity and living a sin-free life, which of course is impossible, we could still not obtain righteousness before God. Remember the law which shows us a need for the Savior. We need only look at the ten commandments and we can see that we have broken God's law of perfection. Have you ever taken God's name in vain? Have you ever disobeyed your parents? Have you ever told a lie or taken something that didn't belong to you? I feel like I needn't go any further. I would guarantee that none of us can say that we aren't guilty of at least one of those.

So, by the standard of perfection, which is God's standard, we cannot be right before God. That is the bad news. However, there is good news. Jesus came to be that righteousness for us. He is righteous and died for us and rose the third day so that anyone who believes on Him won't have to try to earn righteousness or sacrifice an innocent for our guilt. He was the innocent who was sacrificed for our guilt, and ANY of us who believe on Him will be seen right before God.

"By the which will we are sanctified through the offering of the body of Jesus Christ once for all. And every priest standeth daily ministering and offering oftentimes the same sacrifices, which can never take away sins: But this Man (Jesus), after He had offered one sacrifice for sins for ever, sat down on the right hand of God;" (Hebrews 10:10-12) "For He hath made Him to be sin for us, who knew no sin; that we might be made the righteousness of God in Him." (2 Corinthians 5:21)

God will no longer see our sin, but He will see the righteousness of His Son—His innocent blood spilled for us. Like in the garden, he was able to have mercy on the sin of Adam and Eve because of the innocent blood. Though they still had consequences for sin, they weren't immediately killed and thrown into hell. They had punishment, but not damnation.

It is faith in Jesus that brings righteousness because He is righteous. Some will still try to fill that God-sized hole with religion—their own righteousness, but it still leaves one unsatisfied and, without the covering of the blood, condemned or found guilty and damned to hell. "And almost all things are by the law purged with blood; and without shedding of blood is no remission (cancellation of debt/forgiveness)." (Hebrews 9:22)

Paul said this of his brethren, the people of Israel, "For I bear them record that they have a zeal of God, but not according to knowledge. For they being ignorant of God's righteousness, and going about to establish their own righteousness, have not submitted themselves unto the righteousness of God. For Christ is the end of the law for righteousness to every one that believeth." (Romans 10:2-4)

I'm afraid this is the biggest misconception with Christianity. Religion and relationship are different, and God desires the latter.

He wants a relationship with us, and through faith in His Son, Jesus Christ, we can have that relationship. "Therefore being justified by faith, we have peace with God through our Lord Jesus Christ: By whom also we have access by faith into this grace wherein we stand, and rejoice in hope of the glory of God." (Romans 5:1-2)

It is that relationship that brings the first hunger and thirst for righteousness—to be seen right in the eyes of God.

Paul wrote of himself: "And be found in him, not having mine own righteousness, which is of the law, but that which is through the faith of Christ, the righteousness which is of God by faith:" (Philippians 3:9)

As you know when it comes to foods like Brussel sprouts or broccoli even, many people are not fans. However, if you eat these on a regular basis, you will begin to develop a taste for them. Exercise, hard work, and faithfulness may not be natural to us, but when we apply these to our lives on a regular basis, we will develop an appetite for them.

Jesus is called the Bread of Life and the Living Water. These are two of His great "I AM" statements. "And Jesus said unto them, I am the bread of life: he that cometh to me shall never hunger; and he that believeth on me shall never thirst." (John 6:35) Satisfaction is found in Jesus, our righteousness.

We cannot experience this righteousness without first believing in our hearts that He died for our sins, was buried, and rose from the dead three days later. We will then be seen as righteous by God, as He sees the precious blood of His beloved Son when he looks at us who are saved, but that is just a start. That does not automatically give us a hunger for Him, unfortunately. We must feed our soul the Word of God and allow God to nourish us with the words of righteousness.

It is just like that broccoli, for instance. You know it is good for you. You don't like it though, so you eat it once, continue not to like it and never experience the great benefits of having broccoli in your diet. Believers are saved and going to heaven. They have a new nature; however, that new nature needs nourished. We know Bible reading is good for us and that we should attend church to grow and fellowship with other Christians, but we would much rather do the things that we have always done. It seems like too much to pick up for many new Christians.

You won't stop being a Christian if you skip out on those things, but you will miss out on the many blessings that come from knowing Jesus. One of those great blessings is being filled—satisfied—with life no matter what is thrown at you.

We all want to be happy. Satisfaction is happiness—True happiness. "But godliness with contentment is great gain." (1 Timothy 6:6) Appetites are something that can change, but we must be willing to start to feed ourselves some new habits that those good appetites can grow, and we must be willing to starve some of those habits that we may have had an appetite toward for a long time. Remember, it is our hunger and thirst that compel us to action. What do your actions say about your desire (hunger/thirst)?

"O taste and see that the LORD is good: blessed is the man that trusteth in him." (Psalm 34:8)

$$\sim 4 \sim$$

PART II: BIBLICAL EXAMPLE

Zacchaeus, Not Short on Desire to See Jesus

The Bible gives examples of people whose appetites have changed—people who once desired the things of the world, but when they met Jesus and received Him, they began to hunger and thirst after righteousness.

One of those people is Zacchaeus. His story is found in Luke Chapter 19. Zacchaeus was "chief among the publicans, and he was rich." (Luke 19:2) He was the main tax collector in the area and had made a lot of money in it. One thing to know is that the publican/tax collector was hated among the people. They were often crooked and would not only take what they were supposed to take for the government but would also take more to line their pockets. They were cruel thieves. They desired money and would do anything to get it.

That was Zacchaeus' life before he met Jesus, but Zacchaeus was curious and when he heard that Jesus was coming through, he ran to try to see Him, but being as short as Zacchaeus was, he had to climb a tree to get a glimpse of Jesus passing by.

Imagine his amazement when Jesus looked up directly at him and said "Zacchaeus, make haste and come down; for today I must abide at thy house." (Luke 19:5) We don't know what it was that Zacchaeus heard about Jesus. Perhaps it was the amazing miracles that He had performed. Maybe it was the power of His words, the transformed lives of those that He touched, the kindness and compassion that He showed to everyone, even the lowest of the low. We may not know what he heard, but we know that when Jesus called Zacchaeus down from that tree, "he made haste, and came down, and received Him joyfully." (Luke 19:6)

Zacchaeus immediately got down and took Jesus into his home with joy. I believe that he took Jesus into his home and his life. He got saved that day, and there was a difference in his appetites. Zacchaeus being a rich tax collector, again, had a love of money, but once he received Jesus, he had a change of heart. The Bible tells us: "And Zacchaeus stood, and said unto the Lord; Behold, Lord, the half of my goods I give to the poor; and if I have taken any thing from any man by false accusation, I restore him fourfold." (Luke 19:9)

That shows repentance on the part of Zacchaeus. Repentance is needed for salvation. "Testifying both to the Jews, and also to the Greeks, repentance toward God, and faith toward our Lord Jesus Christ." (Acts 20:21)

Repentance is a turning from one thing to another. We are all walking a direction when we meet Jesus. We are walking in the way of the world, but when we get to know the Savior, there should be a turning from that direction to walking with Him in His will. We see this in the life of Zacchaeus. Therefore, Jesus said to him, "This day is salvation come to this house," (Luke 19:9)

We see Zacchaeus went from a hunger and thirst for money to giving money to the poor and he even commits to restoring the things that he had gained through lying. He began to hunger and thirst after righteousness. "For the love of money is the root of all evil: which while some coveted after, they have erred from the faith, and pierced themselves through with many sorrows. But thou, O man of God, flee these things; and follow after righteousness, godliness, faith, love, patience, meekness." (1

Timothy 6:10-11) "But godliness with contentment is great gain." (1 Timothy 6:6)

~ 4 ~

PART II: BIBLICAL EXAMPLE

From Saul to Paul

The apostle Paul wrote about a third of the New Testament. He is known as a spiritual giant, giving us theological truths that we can hold onto and build our lives and relationship with God upon, but Paul was not always on the Lord's side. In fact, Paul, who was known as Saul, was against the followers of Jesus Christ.

When we first see Saul, he is at the stoning of one of Jesus' followers, Steven, who was martyred for his faith. His only crime was preaching truth. Acts chapters six and seven give us a picture of Steven, and at the end of chapter seven, the Bible tells us "Then they cried out with a loud voice, and stopped their ears, and ran upon him with one accord, And cast him out of the city, and stoned him: and the witnesses laid down their clothes at a young man's feet, whose name was Saul." (Acts 7:57-58)

Saul was pleased with this act. He was a one-man terror to the Christian community which was undergoing terrible persecution. "As for Saul, he made havoc of the church, entering into every house, and haling men and women committed them to prison." (Acts 8:3)

Saul did not do these things because he was evil. In his mind, he was doing what was right for the Lord. He was brought up under a great Jewish teacher—went to the best school for preachers, we could say. He was a Pharisee, one of the leaders and teachers of the law.

In Philippians, Paul himself gives an idea of who he may have took pride in before his conversion to Christianity: "Though I might also have confidence in the flesh. If any other man thinketh that he hath whereof he might trust in the flesh, I more: Circumcised the eighth day, of the stock of Israel, of the tribe of Benjamin, an Hebrew of the Hebrews; as touching the law, a Pharisee; Concerning zeal, persecuting the church; touching the righteousness which is in the law, blameless." (Philippians 3:4-6)

Before he knew Christ, he was all about religion and prided himself on being one of the greatest. He considered his acts of terror to be a zeal for God. In fact, many of the religious leaders of that day did.

Interestingly, his name change comes into factor. His name Saul is his Hebrew name. It is the name that would carry all of this stature that he had. Saul means prayed for or desired. I have no doubt that Saul was a prideful man. He was self-righteous. He had a form of godliness but denied the power of God. (2 Timothy 3:5)

The day that Saul met Jesus, none of those things meant anything. You can read about Paul's full conversion in Acts chapter nine. Once Paul got the call from Jesus, he changed completely. Paul went from persecuting the church to going into the church and preaching Jesus as the Son of God. Can you imagine what those Christians did when Paul, the known terrorist, walked into their church as the guest speaker!? "And straightway he [Saul/Paul] preached Christ in the synagogues, that He is the Son of God. But all that heard him were amazed, and said; Is not this he that destroyed them which called on this name in Jerusalem, and came hither for that intent, that he might bring them bound unto the chief priests? But Saul increased the more in strength, and confounded the Jews which dwelt at Damascus, proving that this is very Christ." (Acts 9:20-22)

Paul means small, little or humble, and that is exactly how we see Paul after he meets Jesus. In fact, from that earlier verse where Paul talks about all those things that he could boast in, he goes on to say "But what things were gain to me, those I counted loss for Christ. Yea doubtless, and I count all things but loss for the excellency of the knowledge of Christ Jesus my Lord: for whom I have suffered the loss of all things, and do count them but dung, that I may win Christ, And be found in him, not having mine own righteousness, which is of the law, but that which is through the faith of Christ, the righteousness which is of God by faith:" (Philippians 3:7-9)

He went from praising his righteousness to praising God's righteousness and from a desire to live by the law and please the leaders of the day to a desire to live by grace and please Jesus in all that he did. In fact, those religious leaders wanted to kill Paul after his conversion.

There is no denying that Paul changed. His desires changed. What satisfied him changed. Those things from before that he held to be so precious, he counted as dung! What an example! Truthfully, everything that we valued before Christ is dung compared to Him and the life that He has for us.

Zacchaeus and Paul may have looked like they had it all to the world; both were rich and had status. However, when they saw Jesus, those things didn't look so shiny anymore. Their hunger and thirst changed to Jesus. They found fulfillment in His calling.

Have you found fulfillment in the calling of Christ? What do you desire most in this world? The Word of God tells us: "And when He had called the people unto Him with His disciples also, He said unto them, Whosoever will come after me, let him deny himself, and take up his cross, and follow me. For whosoever will save his life shall lose it; but whosoever shall lose his life for My sake and the gospel's, the same shall save it. For what shall it profit a man, if he shall gain the whole world, and lose his own soul? Or what shall a man give in exchange for his soul?" (Mark 8:34-37)

Think about that! If we are going to follow Christ, we must be willing to deny ourselves. Remember, broccoli doesn't taste great to everyone at first. Exercise is really hard for we who have put it away for a few years. However, we know these things are good for us and we will develop an appetite if we start feeding ourselves with these great habits of eating vegetables and exercising.

It is the same with spending time with the Savior. It seems like it is taking a lot of extra time to read the Bible and pray and go to church at least once a week. Truth is, if you add up the time, I guarantee it isn't anything you can't put into your schedule. You will be surprised how much you can get to know Jesus in five minutes—if you'd set aside the time, and then allow that to grow and grow as the desire grows.

"The stiff and wooden quality about our religious lives is a result of our lack of holy desire. Complacency is a deadly foe of all spiritual growth. Acute desire must be present or there will be no manifestation of Christ to His people." -A.W. Tozer

~ 4 ~

PART III: PERSONAL EXAMPLE

I remember when my desires changed from child-like desires to that teenage, not-an-adult-but-not-a-child phase. I wish I could say that I desired hard work and good grades, but the freshman year of high school brought on depression, so my only desire was to get rid of my feelings.

That was the year when I turned to disastrous desires that would affect me for the next eighteen years of my life. Some years were worse than others, but there were very few days where I wasn't smoking weed or drinking alcohol, except when I was pregnant.

I had a hunger and thirst for the covering in the moment that the drugs gave me. I could ignore my feelings and circumstances. Of course, the next day those things were still there and because I hadn't dealt with them, they only got worse, so the endless cycle continued.

I desired peace and marijuana falsely provided that. I desired to be accepted and being able to get alcohol when many people couldn't got me "friends" quickly. I desired happiness and being surrounded by people gave the illusion that I was happy—that I was accepted. My drug-induced smile covered the sadness in my soul.

Day after day and year after year, I had the same desires and tried the same quick fixes that never really provided what I was longing for. It wasn't until that day in January 2013 when I just couldn't pretend anymore.

At that point of my life, there was rarely a day when our family didn't have a visitor. I had marijuana and alcohol every day if I wanted it—and I did. Yet, that covering was not doing the job anymore. I had a stinging pain inside and a voice in my head that told me that everyone would be better without me.

I fought against that voice and called out to God. It had been a long time since I called out to Him and even longer since I called out to Him sincerely; yet He heard me that day. I was surprised that He paid attention me. I was even more surprised that He answered me.

Do you know what happened as I called out to God? He sent one of His people to contact me and invite me to church. At that point, it had been possibly three weeks since I had been clean —no weed, alcohol, or cigarettes. I was five or six weeks pregnant. Though I didn't have those things because of my unborn child, I still desired them. I still wanted that covering that they provided. Even more, I wanted the peace, acceptance, and happiness that provided a semblance to my reality.

One thing changed right away though. I had a hunger and thirst for the Word of God. I began to read my Bible as part of the ladies' fellowship, and I fell in love with it. As I started the RU Program, I got even deeper into the Word of God, and going to church and reading my Bible began to fill those longings that the weed and alcohol had covered for so long.

I knew acceptance as I had never known it in my entire life. God knew everything about me—everything! Yet, He loved me anyway, died for my sins and desired a relationship with me. That blew my mind! And it still does today! I no longer needed to be surrounded by people who were never truly interested in me.

Unfortunately, I had a miscarriage only a month or so into my Christian walk. It was hard in so many ways. I wanted that baby. My children wanted that little brother or sister. We embraced the idea of a super large family. The loss was real to us, though he/she wasn't born yet. However, I now can know that one day I will see that little one in heaven.

At that time, such a hard blow would've usually drawn me back to the weed and alcohol, but I didn't have the desire to go there. I was filled—satisfied. Amen! I had those things that I was trying to imitate with things that didn't satisfy. I had peace. It hurt that I lost my baby, but I had peace about it. I trusted God in it.

I had acceptance, not only with my God, but with my new family of God. My church family was supportive, helpful, and embraced me right where I was. I was beginning to know happiness—true happiness.

The more that I gained knowledge through Bible study, church services and fellowship with fellow believers, the more I was fulfilled in my life. I began to work in the children's ministry which brought even more fulfillment. My hunger and thirst became more about God and His kingdom than any of the things that I held of high esteem before.

I didn't have to think about what sins I needed to put away; they naturally dropped away from my life. Now, not all of them. I still have struggles. I will always have struggles. In fact, I have struggles that I don't even know that I have yet. Understand that God never gives us more than we can handle, and there is no way any human can work on all their "stuff" at one time. However, because my hunger and thirst has changed, these struggles are merely weeds that I need to pull up as I walk through life. They aren't a jungle of big hinderances because I can see them as they grow up. God sheds light on them.

When my hunger and thirst are after the things of the world, those struggles are no longer little, but they become boulders in my path that prevent me from moving forward for the Lord.

So, it is important that one of the desires that we allow to grow in our lives is the Word of God. Like I said, I was still living for the world when I first went to church. I didn't know Paul from Peter. I didn't understand what my entertainment was doing to my soul. However, when I got into the Word of God, over time, God shed light on what was in front of me—little by little—and helped me to turn away from things that were boulders in my path. He gave me different music that I enjoy. I enjoy reading my Bible for entertainment. I can find pleasure in shows that aren't blaspheming my God or turning my heart away from Him. I find joy in serving God.

It was God that changed my desires, not me. I had tried time and time again to "quit smoking, quit drinking, quit cussing..." He changed my mind about things—it was His Word with its transforming power. How often do you read the Word of God and truly think about it? "For the word of God is quick, and powerful, and sharper than any twoedged sword, piercing even to the dividing asunder of soul and spirit, and of the joints and marrow, and is a discerner of the thoughts and intents of the heart." (Hebrews 4:12)

~ 4 ~

PART IV: GO DEEPER

1. What does hunger and thirst mean?

____

____

2. What is righteousness?

____

____

3. Where does righteousness come from? How can we be righteous?

____

____

____

4. What did you hunger and thirst for before you knew Christ?

____

____

____

____

5. Since knowing Christ as your personal Savior (I'm assuming you do. If you don't, please see the appendix for how you can know Jesus as your personal Savior.), what desires do you have? Any new desires?

____

____

----

6. Compare your desires and the outcome they brought before Christ and after Christ. Take note of these things so that when you begin to desire those old things again, you can remember the fruit (outcome) of those things.

----

7. Write some of those old desires that you still crave often. Look up at least two verses about what God's Word says about each of them and write them down. Take time to look at these verses, study them, think about them, memorize, and meditate on them. Also, replace that desire with something godly.

----

8. Consider these verses: That ye put off concerning the former conversation the old man, which is corrupt according to the deceitful lusts; And be renewed in the spirit of your mind; And that ye put on the new man, which after God is created in righteousness and true holiness. Wherefore putting away lying, speak every man truth with his neighbour: for we are members one of another. Be ye angry, and sin not: let not the sun go down upon your wrath: Neither give place to the devil. Let him that stole steal no more: but rather let him labour, working with his hands the thing which is good, that he may have to give to him that needeth. Let no corrupt communication proceed out of your mouth, but that which is good to the use of edifying, that it may minister grace unto the hearers. And grieve not the holy Spirit of God, whereby ye are sealed unto the day of redemption. Let all bitterness, and wrath, and anger, and clamour, and evil speaking, be put away from you, with all malice: And be ye kind one to another, tenderhearted, forgiving

one another, even as God for Christ's sake hath forgiven you."
(Ephesians 4:22-32)

    a. When we put off something, we should put on something else:

      i. When we put off our old nature, what should we put on (Ephesians 4:24)

----

      ii. How do we do that according to Ephesians 4:23?

----

     iii. If we stop lying, what should we replace it with, according to Ephesians 4:25?

----

     iv. If we stop stealing, what should we replace it with according to Ephesians 4:28?

----

     v. What should we stop according to Ephesians 4:29? What should it be replaced with? Why? (all found in v. 29)

----

     vi. Ephesians 4:32 tells us to put away all bitterness, wrath, anger, clamor, and evil speaking with malice. What is malice?

----

     vii. What should we replace those things in Ephesians 4:32 with according to Ephesians 4:33? Why?

~ 5 ~

BLESSED ARE THE MERCIFUL

"Blessed are the merciful: for they shall obtain mercy." (Matthew 5:7)

Part I—Insight: Gaining Knowledge

Mercy is another one of those characteristics that the world considers to be a weakness. The definition of mercy is active compassion. Websters 1828 dictionary gives a more specific definition —benevolence, mildness or tenderness of heart which disposes a person to overlook injuries, or to treat an offender better than he deserves. Simply, one might say that mercy is not getting what you deserve.

We all can surely understand how receiving mercy can make us happy; it is the giving of mercy that we might have trouble with. When someone wrongs us or someone that we care about, it is natural to want that person to "get what he deserves," and, of course, we feel like we are the ones who can choose what that person deserves. So, often, we don't consider mercy at all and jump to our own system of judgment.

Have you ever been wronged, jumped to conclusions, and hurt the wrong person in your retaliation? I know I have. That is just one simple reason why we shouldn't take judgment into our own hands.

Of course, Jesus always has deeper reasons. "Dearly beloved, avenge not yourselves, but rather give place unto wrath: for it is written, Vengeance is mine; I will repay, saith the Lord." (Romans 12:9)

Mercy is at the heart of the gospel. It is an act of love from God. See, because of our sin, we deserve the punishment of death and hell. We deserve separation from God for eternity. "For the wages of sin is death;" (Romans 6:23a) Can we deny that we are sinners? Can we then deny that we owe death? The answer should be no to both of those questions.

"What then? are we better than they? No, in no wise: for we have before proved both Jews and Gentiles, that they are **all** under sin; As it is written, There is **none righteous**, no, not one: There is **none** that understandeth, there is **none** that seeketh after God. They are **all** gone out of the way, they are together become unprofitable; there is **none** that doeth good, no, **not one**." (Romans 3:9-12) "For all have sinned, and come short of the glory of God;" (Romans 3:23)

God knows we are all unworthy. God knows we have denied Him over and over again. Yet, He still loves us and showed His love by sending His only begotten Son to die for our sins. "For God so loved the world, that he gave his only begotten Son, that whosoever believeth in him should not perish, but have everlasting life." (John 3:16)

See, we owed death and Jesus paid it for us. He paid our sin debt with His life. Amazingly, He did it while we were sinners and knowing that many would still choose sin over Him. "But God commendeth his love toward us, in that, while we were yet sinners, Christ died for us." (Romans 5:8)

This is love! This is grace! This is mercy! And why? Why did God show such love, grace, and mercy? So that some would choose Him. "We love Him, because He first loved us." (1 John 4:19)

Throughout the entire Bible, you can see this amazing love story of how God continually showed mercy and grace to His people and his enemies. He did it to show that He is different. From the first rebellion in the Garden of Eden when Adam and Eve sinned, He showed that active compassion by killing an innocent animal for His beloved creation—mankind.

Even as Cain killed his righteous brother, Abel, God had mercy on Cain and did not allow others to get revenge on him. It was not yet an established law that murder was a crime and so God didn't allow that vengeance; however, he did bring punishment upon Cain. *There are always consequences for our sin, even with God's mercy.*

In the midst of global judgment, God made a way that anyone who would believe what He said, through the preaching of Noah, could be saved. However, no one besides Noah's family believed. When Jonah tried to run away from God, he was given a second chance in the belly of a large fish. Consider this, Jonah was on his way to give the gospel to the most wicked nation at that time—Nineveh, the capital of Assyria, and they believed what God said and received mercy! Time and time again, God showed His mercy...so that we will choose Him.

Now that we have chosen Him—prayerfully you have accepted the free gift of salvation available to all who will believe that Jesus died for your sins, was buried and rose the third day—we are to show mercy to others. Why? First, because we have received mercy. Remember every one of these be-attitudes are a positional attitude. It is **because** we have inherited the kingdom of heaven that we are poor in spirit. It is because we are comforted that we mourn over our sin. It is **because** we inherit the earth that we are meek. It is **because** we are satisfied (filled) that we hunger and thirst after righteousness. And it is **because** we have obtained mercy that we are merciful.

"Put on therefore, as the elect of God, holy and beloved, bowels of mercies, kindness, humbleness of mind, meekness, longsuffering; Forbearing one another, and forgiving one another, if any man have a quarrel against any: even as Christ forgave you, so also do ye." (Colossians 3:12-13)

"Put on therefore" means to clothe yourself accordingly—let this be what people see when they look at you. "As the elect of God" indicates the reason you would clothe yourself accordingly—you have been chosen by God and have accepted the call to be a child of God.

"Holy and beloved." This is positional again. We are chosen by God and have accepted His call and therefore we are holy and beloved. We are set apart unto Him and loved dearly. All are chosen and called by God. It is then up to us to choose to accept that invitation into His family. Also, we are all loved by God. He sent His Son to die for the sins of the world. "And He is the propitiation for our sins: and not for ours only, but also for the sins of the whole world." (1 John 2:2) What a shame that many will not choose Him!

The verse goes on to tell us what we are to be clothed in—bowels of mercies. "Bowels" refers to an inward affection and "mercies" is meaning mercy, that willingness to choose not to give someone what they deserve—to forgive and have pity or compassion on someone.

Again, because God is so merciful to us and daily overlooks our shortcomings and loads us with blessings, we should do the same for others—not that we would get anything in return, but that the person to whom we showed mercy would see God in us and turn to Him. "Blessed be the Lord, who daily loadeth us with benefits, even the God of our salvation. Selah." (Psalm 68:19)

Mercy is more than just overlooking an offense. It is also showing compassion to a person who is in need. That is how God saw us—in need. Yes, we had sinned against Him and deserved eternal punishment—still deserve eternal punishment. However, in His love and mercy, He sent His Son to die in our place. "Verily, verily, I say unto you, He that heareth my word, and believeth on Him that sent me, hath everlasting life, and shall not come into condemnation; but is passed from death unto life." (John 5:24)

Also, though, we were in need. We were lost. We were without this great love. We were without peace and hope. We were without life in our spirits. We needed a Savior.

Many people are hurting. They are lost. They are without His great love. They lack peace and hope, and they walk around without life in their spirits. This can be manifest in many ways, and we are not to judge but to love. We are to show the world who Jesus is by showing who He has been to us. It is not only good for those for whom we show compassion. It will bring happiness in our lives as well as you will see with the Biblical examples below.

We often overlook the one who never has peace and is always complaining. We would rather avoid the person who always needs help and refuses every invite to church and conversation about the Lord. We can get uncomfortable with the sick and dying. However, all of these people and many others who need Jesus need us to show mercy—that active compassion—to them so that some will choose Him. It's our calling—to walk as Jesus walked. "And Jesus, when he came out, saw much people, and was moved with compassion toward them, because they were as sheep not having a shepherd: and he began to teach them many things." (Matthew 6:34) How many people don't know Jesus but know you?!

Do we even see those who need mercy anymore? "Blessed are the merciful: for they shall obtain mercy." (Matthew 5:7) We already received mercy. I want to explain that these beatitudes are not a magic formula that if I give mercy, that mercy will be returned to me. Unfortunately, like every characteristic that God gives us, many will not choose it. Even many of the children of God have left off mercy. Perhaps they get tired in welldoing because they do not see results. However, God is working. When we will choose His way, there are mountains moving. He often returns mercy through other people or He Himself shows up in your life. We might not see it, though, until we get to heaven, but know that God is working. However, we do not give mercy to receive mercy. We have mercy, so we should freely give it to others.

~ 5 ~

PART II: BIBLICAL EXAMPLE

Nabal, Abigail and David

(1 Samuel 25)

Like the previous illustration, we see that mercy is seeing a need and having compassion on that one in need and providing that person with the need. They can't always give back, but God will return what we sacrifice. "He that hath pity upon the poor lendeth unto the LORD; and that which he hath given will he pay him again." (Proverbs 19:17)

Mercy is also that forgiveness—that overlooking an offense and not giving someone what they "deserve" but allowing God to judge afflictions and oppression. In the passage of scripture that we look at today, we see three people in the midst of one problem. We will look at what a lack of mercy can do and how mercy can pacify a wrong spirit within someone and turn them to God.

In this part of history that we're looking at in 1 Samuel 25, David was a young man who was not yet king. He had already been anointed as the next king of Israel, and the king at the time, Saul, had wanted him dead. So, David was on the run. He had very little except for his love for God, his kindness to others, and his trusted men who stayed with him.

David had found himself in Paran where a rich man, Nabal, had shepherds doing business. David and his men looked after the shepherds and protected them from thieves. However, David and his men were hungry and thirsty, and David sent word to Nabal to ask for mercy—for him to have compassion on them. He asked, not as charity but because he looked after his men and supplies.

"And David sent out ten young men, and David said unto the young men, Get you up to Carmel, and go to Nabal, and greet him in my name: And thus shall ye say to him that liveth in prosperity, Peace be both to thee, and peace be to thine house, and peace be unto all that thou hast. And now I have heard that thou hast shearers: now thy shepherds which were with us, we hurt them not, neither was there ought missing unto them, all the while they were in Carmel. Ask thy young men, and they will shew thee. Wherefore let the young men find favour in thine eyes: for we come in a good day: give, I pray thee, whatsoever cometh to thine hand unto thy servants, and to thy son David. And when David's young men came, they spake to Nabal according to all those words in the name of David, and ceased. (1 Samuel 25:5-9)

Notice the humility of the future king. He entreats Nabal with kindness and he asks for anything that Nabal would find acceptable to give.

What was the response of Nabal? "And Nabal answered David's servants, and said, Who is David? and who is the son of Jesse? there be many servants now a days that break away every man from his master. Shall I then take my bread, and my water, and my flesh that I have killed for my shearers, and give it unto men, whom I know not whence they be?" (1 Samuel 25:10-11)

Nabal's response was harsh. The Bible calls him "churlish and evil in his doings..." (1 Samuel 25:3) Churlish means cruel and stubborn. There is little doubt that Nabal had not heard of David. He was a captain of king Saul's army. It was said that while Saul had killed thousands, David had killed tens of thousands (1 Samuel 18:7). He was anointed to be the next king of Israel—Nabal's next king as he "was of the house of Caleb." (1 Samuel 25:3)

Nabal showed himself to be prideful and cruel as he refused to give even a little to men who had protected his interests. He in no way showed mercy and this angered David. David intended to bring war to the house of Nabal. "And David said unto his men, Gird ye on every man his sword. And they girded on every man his sword; and David also girded on his sword: and there went up after David about four hundred men; and two hundred abode by the stuff." (1 Samuel 25:13)

Should Nabal have given of the plenteous goods that he had? Absolutely! "But whoso hath this world's good, and seeth his brother have need, and shutteth up his bowels of compassion from him, how dwelleth the love of God in him?" (1 John 3:17)

However, was Nabal's rudeness reason to go to war? I would say no. David's response to the lack of mercy of Nabal was just as bad, and without mercy this part of history would've been bad for the house of Nabal and for David, but mercy stepped in.

Nabal had a kind, God-fearing wife and one of Nabal's servants went to her and told her what had happened. "But one of the young men told Abigail, Nabal's wife, saying, Behold, David sent messengers out of the wilderness to salute our master; and he railed on them. But the men were very good unto us, and we were not hurt, neither missed we any thing, as long as we were conversant with them, when we were in the fields: They were a wall unto us both by night and day, all the while we were with them keeping the sheep. Now therefore know and consider what thou wilt do; for evil is determined against our master, and against all his household: for he is such a son of Belial, that a man cannot speak to him. (1 Samuel 25:14-17)

Abigail immediately went and gathered up some food and bolted toward where David was. She was bold as she approached the wrathful, determinate David. She bowed to him and began to plead for mercy for her husband's foolish response as she extended mercy with the goods she brought to them. (1 Samuel 25:18-24) "Let not my lord, I pray thee, regard this man of Belial, even Nabal: for as his name is, so is he; Nabal is his name, and folly is with him: but I thine handmaid saw not the young men of my lord, whom thou didst send. Now therefore, my lord, as the LORD liveth, and as thy soul liveth, seeing the LORD hath withholden thee from coming to shed blood, and from avenging thyself with thine own hand, now let thine enemies, and they that seek evil to my lord, be as Nabal. And now this blessing which thine handmaid hath brought unto my lord, let it even be given unto the young men that follow my lord. I pray thee, forgive the trespass of thine handmaid: for the LORD will certainly make my lord a sure house; because my lord fighteth the battles of the LORD, and evil hath not been found in thee all thy days." (1 Samuel 25:25-28)

David had a choice to make, and he made the right choice. He accepted the mercy of Abigail, Nabal's wife, and he also chose to have mercy on Nabal and his house. "And David said to Abigail, Blessed be the LORD God of Israel, which sent thee this day to meet me: And blessed be thy advice, and blessed be thou, which hast kept me this day from coming to shed blood, and from avenging myself with mine own hand. For in very deed, as the LORD God of Israel liveth, which hath kept me back from hurting thee, except thou hadst hasted and come to meet me, surely there had not been left unto Nabal by the morning light any that pisseth against the wall. So David received of her hand that which she had brought him, and said unto her, Go up in peace to thine house; see, I have hearkened to thy voice, and have accepted thy person." (1 Samuel 25:32-35)

David recognizes where this mercy comes from—yes, it was from Abigail, but it was also from the LORD God. David was not in his right mind to go to war. That was not the response that God would've wanted from him. He responded in his flesh and not with the mercy that he was given daily by God. Abigail's mercy reminded David of God's mercy which caused him to then show mercy to Nabal. "Blessed are the merciful: for they shall obtain mercy." (Matthew 5:7)

~ 5 ~

PART II: BIBLICAL EXAMPLE

The Widow Woman

(1 Kings 17:8-24)

In 1st Kings we see a widow woman in the city of Zarephath. Families with no man were and still are important to God. While today we have much opportunity to provide for our families, whether male or female, in the time before Christ, there was very little opportunity for a woman to provide. They relied on their husbands; therefore, God often gave commandment for the children of God to watch for and take care of the widows and fatherless.

In the giving of the Law, God commanded: "Ye shall not afflict any widow, or fatherless child. If thou afflict them in any wise, and they cry at all unto me, I will surely hear their cry;" (Exodus 22:22-23) In the New Testament, James reiterates this truth: "Pure religion and undefiled before God and the Father is this, To visit the fatherless and widows in their affliction, and to keep himself unspotted from the world." (James 1:27)

God had made it clear that if you love Him, you will care for—have mercy upon—those who are widows and fatherless. However, in our text today, God sent the man of God, Elijah, to this widow to lodge with her and be fed by her. "And the word of the LORD came unto him, saying, Arise, get thee to Zarephath, which belongeth to

Zidon, and dwell there: behold, I have commanded a widow woman there to sustain thee." (1 Kings 17:8-9)

There was a drought in the land—no water. Elijah had been provided water by the brook Cherith and food by the ravens, but the brook had dried up and God left off commanding the ravens to feed him. He was in a dire position, but he trusted God and did what God said.

As he went to Zarephath, he immediately ran into the widow woman who was in a dire position herself. She was gathering sticks together to make her and her son their last meal.

Elijah, following God's command and unaware of her state, asks for water and the woman went to receive it for him, but as she was moved to help him, he asked further of some bread. There was where Elijah was told just how desperate the woman was. "And she said, As the LORD thy God liveth, I have not a cake, but an handful of meal in a barrel, and a little oil in a cruse: and, behold, I am gathering two sticks, that I may go in and dress it for me and my son, that we may eat it, and die." (1 Kings 17:12)

Again, there was a drought and that widow woman was preparing her last meal for her and her son. You may think that Elijah would have pity on her—show her mercy, but he also had nothing. He was just following God and trusting Him. So, his response: "And Elijah said unto her, Fear not; go and do as thou hast said: but make me thereof a little cake first, and bring it unto me, and after make for thee and for thy son." (1 Kings 17:13)

Can you imagine the widow woman's face? "What!," she may have been thinking. "I am making this last meal and you want me to feed you first?!" That's what we might have thought. And we may have answered "No way!" However, that is not what we see in this widow woman. In fact, from the time that Elijah encountered her, she had shown mercy.

Before she could respond, Elijah told her what God had said: "For thus saith the LORD God of Israel, The barrel of meal shall not waste, neither shall the cruse of oil fail, until the day that the LORD sendeth rain upon the earth." (1 Kings 17:14)

God had promised provision. Although there was a drought, although she was at the very last of her food, although she then had another mouth to feed, God said that as long as she provided Elijah with food, she and her son would have food as well.

The widow woman believed God. "And she went and did according to the saying of Elijah: and she, and he, and her house, did eat many days." (1 Kings 17:15) So, how was she rewarded? What happiness befell her obedience to be merciful? "And the barrel of meal wasted not, neither did the cruse of oil fail, according to the word of the LORD, which he spake by Elijah." (1 Kings 17:16)

What an example of mercy! That woman was at her last and she could've been selfish. She could've relied on her own understanding, but instead she trusted God. Mercy requires us to trust God.

He often sends us into situations that don't make sense to our natural mind. Just think about this one situation. It made no sense that a poor widow woman and her son who were on their last meal would take in a stranger and feed him.

The next time God tells us to give to someone when we feel like we have very little to give, let us remember this widow woman and her mercy. Let us also trust God and not rely on our own understanding. Who knows what blessing we may receive; however, I warn that we don't do it for the blessing. Let us always trust God and follow Him because we love Him not because of what we can get from Him. "Let not mercy and truth forsake thee: bind them about thy neck; write them upon the table of thine heart: So shalt thou find favour and good understanding in the sight of God and man. Trust in the LORD with all thine heart; and lean not unto thine own understanding. In all thy ways acknowledge him, and he shall direct thy paths. Be not wise in thine own eyes: fear the LORD, and depart from evil." (Proverbs 3:4-7)

~ 5 ~

PART III: PERSONAL EXAMPLE

Wednesday, January 30th, 2013, I needed mercy. I needed someone to look on me with compassion and love me right where I was. That's exactly what I found in my Savior, Jesus Christ. I had nothing to give. I wasn't even sure if I could give myself. I was at the end of me and desired to be in a different place. I no longer wanted to be tired, anxious, depressed, and filled with anger. I no longer wanted to think about ending my life. I wanted peace above all things.

That cold afternoon when I called out to God, I wasn't necessarily expecting an answer. I had called out to God many times. I had wanted God to get me out of a tough situation that seemed very harmful to me. I even promised that I would change my life if he got me out of it. However, that Wednesday afternoon things were different. I was different.

I wasn't really in a tough situation—at least in my mind, I didn't think so. My main prayer was that I would stop wanting to die so I could be here for my kids.

When God answered by sending Judi Meyer to call me and invite me to church the next day, I can't explain how I felt His presence. I had a calm that I didn't even recognize until a couple of weeks later. That call changed me. Not necessarily because of Mrs. Judi, though she was an intricate part in it. It was because God heard my cry and answered me. That brought hope that I didn't have before.

I am not sure when I accepted Jesus as my Savior. It could've been that moment. It could've been when I was 11 years old at a Vacation Bible School when I talked with a merciful teacher at what is now Martins Ferry Christian School. I feel like that was a life-altering moment for me and it would explain my turmoil in my youth, teen years, and young adult years as I spent no time trying to live for God.

One thing I know for sure is that by that next week after that Ladies Fellowship that Thursday—two Sundays following—I had no doubt that I believed in God with my whole heart, and I trusted Him to save my soul from hell and to change my life and do something great. I surrendered my life to Him that day.

What mercy He showed me by meeting me right where I was! He did not condemn me. He did not push me away. He held me and comforted me and told me that He loves me and will never leave me nor forsake me. He spoke through His Word and through His people.

God's love and mercy changed me. Before even knowing much and not knowing if what I knew was the truth or not, I instinctively wanted to tell others and that is what I started doing. I went home and told my boyfriend at the time who was in the process of leaving. I told my kids, my mom, my siblings, my nanna, aunts, cousins, friends, neighbors...anyone who was around me knew that there was something different, even if I didn't say it.

God began to teach me how to deal with people in love, and He is still teaching me this today. He started to make clear some errors in judgment that I had with my boyfriend and children.

With great struggles, I attempted to correct those errors in judgment. My boyfriend thought I had gotten "religion" and thought that I was better than him. My children who were ages 13, 9, 8, 6, 4 and 3 embraced the new me and they seemed to develop a love for the Word and Jesus just as I did.

Week after week, my children and I would go to church. We would have bible studies at home and sing some of the new songs we were learning on the church van. My boyfriend was still considering leaving, but God gave me great grace and mercy in dealing with him and I could see him softening.

It was about a month after first attending that Patrick, Sr. decided to join us to church. Without going into detail, I am telling you that it was mercy that enabled him to want to go to church. He had made it very difficult to live with him during that month. It was like fighting demons whenever he was home, and for me to be able to be any way except angry was the mercy of God. I have no doubt that it was that mercy that Patrick saw in me that made him want to go to church. He has even said so.

In just two weeks of attending church and hearing the gospel, he got saved. Our family was on a new path. Within that first year our oldest daughter got saved and we decided to fully commit to each other in marriage. What a difference a year made! And it was all because of mercy. God first showing me mercy and teaching me what mercy is and then a choice to yield to Him that I could be merciful to others.

It was, of course, not all peaches and sunshine for our family. We have had much heartache, tribulation, and persecution from following Christ; however, mercy has been extended to others, and others have come to Christ or at least made a profession of faith since that. All of my children, even my now seven-year-old has made a profession of faith. Every one of my immediate family members and every first cousin of mine who lives in this area has come to church because of the mercy that God extended and many of them made professions of faith. Several friends have chosen to go to church and heard the gospel, some believing. Why? Because someone cared—someone showed mercy. Someone was changed by the mercy that they received and began to show it to them.

Although it is God's desire to use mercy to turn others to Him, not all people will accept mercy. I have had relationships with what others may call "difficult,"—those who seem to only want what they want when they want it and not interested in real help from Jesus and the truth found in His Word. God put me in those relationships to show His mercy where others couldn't. While I have seen great strides in a couple friends, there are others who I've seen little growth and yet others who have never accepted the mercy of God. Sadly, some have met eternity without knowing Him. However, those with whom I had a relationship are without excuse because God's mercy was made known to them.

We can't know how mercy will affect any person, but we can know that it is God's plan for us to show mercy to others, whether it is that forebearance and kindness that overlooks offenses or that compassion that meets people's needs even though they have little to nothing to return. Mercy is a great factor in His calling people to repentance.

"Happy are those whose self-centered lives have been crushed and reshaped by the Master's hand to be full of mercy." — John Hagee

"Your Lord is a God of mercy and bountifulness: be a source of mercy and bountifulness to your neighbors. If you will be such, you will find salvation yourself with everlasting glory." —John of Kronstadt

~ 5 ~

PART IV: GO DEEPER

1. What is mercy?

----

2. Why should you give mercy to others?

----

3. Read the following passage and answer the questions that follow:

"Then came Peter to him, and said, Lord, how oft shall my brother sin against me, and I forgive him? till seven times? Jesus saith unto him, I say not unto thee, Until seven times: but, Until seventy times seven. Therefore is the kingdom of heaven likened unto a certain king, which would take account of his servants. And when he had begun to reckon, one was brought unto him, which owed him ten thousand talents. But forasmuch as he had not to pay, his lord commanded him to be sold, and his wife, and children, and all that he had, and payment to be made. The servant therefore fell down, and worshipped him, saying, Lord, have patience with me, and I will pay thee all. Then the lord of that servant was moved with compassion, and loosed him, and forgave him the debt. But the same servant went out, and found one of his fellowservants, which owed him an hundred pence: and he laid hands on him, and took him by the throat, saying, Pay me that thou owest. And his fellowservant fell down at his feet, and besought him, saying, Have patience with me, and I will pay thee all. And he would not: but went and cast him into prison, till he should pay the debt. So when his fellowservants saw what was done, they were very sorry, and came and told unto their lord all that was done. Then his lord, after that he had called him, said unto him, O thou wicked servant, I forgave thee all that debt, because thou desiredst me: Shouldest not thou also have had compassion on thy fellowservant, even as I had pity on thee? And his lord was wroth, and delivered him to the tormentors, till he should pay all that was due unto him. So likewise shall my heavenly Father do also unto you, if ye from your hearts forgive not every one his brother their trespasses. (Matthew 18:21-35)

a. How many times did Jesus tell Peter to forgive?

----

b. What do you think that means when we think about mercy?

----

c. Who do you think the king in this story represents?

----

d. Who do you think the servants represent?

----

e. Why was the first servant going be sold into slavery along with his family?

----

f. How did that servant respond to the king/lord?

----

g. What was the king's response to the first servant after that?

---

h. If you had to define the king using some character traits, what would be a few that you would say? Is merciful one of them?

---

i. What did that servant (the first one) do when he realized that another servant owed him money?

---

j. How did you respond to that first servant when reading his response with the other servant? Why?

---

k. His other fellow-servants were very upset with him and reported him to the king who "delivered him to the tormentors." Do you consider this response harsh? Why or why not?

---

l. A parable means an earthly story with a heavenly meaning. Jesus is talking about something deeper than a king and his servants. He is talking about Himself and the kingdom of God and the believers. We have been greatly forgiven, shown the greatest mercies each day, but often we go about our days forgetting about those mercies when we deal with others. May we learn from this parable. Jesus takes how we treat other people very seriously if we are going to claim His name.

m. What is your biggest takeaway from this parable?

____

____

____

____

____

____

4. How has God's mercy affected your behavior toward others?

____

____

____

____

____

____

5. Has anyone treated you with mercy (forgiven you or took you in and fed you/clothed you, spent time with you when you could offer nothing in return—perhaps you even were ungrateful and didn't even thank them or weren't kind in return)? If so, has that mercy affected you in any way?

____

____

____

____

____

____

6. When was the last time that you showed true mercy to someone? Write about that time. What was the response of that person whom you had mercy upon? Were there any blessings received from that mercy that you gave? If you can't think of a time, choose to show mercy this week to someone. Reach out to someone you've been avoiding because they seem "needy" and be there for them. Give of your time or goods to the poor. Forgive someone of a grudge or pain that you have not let go of (this will release you too,

but you will need God's help with it). Write about that experience. Did it bring happiness?

~ 6 ~

BLESSED ARE THE PURE IN HEART: FOR THEY SHALL SEE GOD

Part I—INSIGHT: Gaining Knowledge

"Blessed are the pure in heart: for they shall see God." (Matthew 5:8)

Pure means free from moral defilement; without spot; not sullied or tarnished; incorrupt; undebased by moral turpitude; holy. I feel like that definition needs defined. Moral means concerned with the principles of right and wrong behavior and the goodness or badness of human character. Defilement is pollution. The rest of the words in the definition carry this same idea of not being polluted in what is right and wrong and what is good and bad. Holy means set apart unto a sacred use. Heart is referring to our thoughts, emotions, and desires—it is the core of our being that motivates every decision that we make.

Supremely happy are those who have no pollution/poison/impurities in their thoughts, emotions, and desires—those who have allowed themselves to be set apart for God unto sacred use. For or because they shall see God. To see means to gaze (that is, with wide open eyes, as at something remarkable). Interestingly this word see used in this instance holds that it differs from some other uses of the word "see": It is not a passive see God. It is a recognition

93

of seeing God as God. God, of course referring to the Supreme God...the One True God, Jehovah, the self-existent One who brings salvation to all who will believe on His Son.

Purity of heart does not come from anything that we do on our own. It comes from salvation, a trust in the finished work of Jesus on the cross. It is His blood that brings purity to our hearts, and it is His work, day by day, that will sanctify and continue to work on our hearts to keep our hearts clean and grow us to be more and more like Him.

On its own, the heart is deceitful above all things and desperately wicked that we can't even know it (Jeremiah 17:9). We will not even notice the impurity of our heart without the new nature that Jesus gives us at our second birth. Again, the heart, as mentioned in the Bible, consists of our thoughts, feelings, and desires. It is who we are.

For our entire lives, until we come to trust in Jesus as our Savior, we are led by thoughts, feelings, and desires that are consistent with the world around us and the philosophies of the present culture. From Jeremiah 17:9, we can gather that we are blinded through-out this time by lies ("deceitful above all things") and wickedness ("desperately wicked"). Yet, I don't know about you, but I never thought of myself as a wicked person. To me, a murderer or a rapist would be considered a wicked person, but not a person going about her life just trying to do her best. Wrong!

I didn't realize that I was wrong until I met Jesus. "Therefore if any man be in Christ, he is a new creature: old things are passed away; behold, all things are become new." (2 Corinthians 5:17) While we still have that old heart at salvation, we are given a new nature and our spirit comes alive to where we can now communicate with God. Therefore, even one who was a murderer or a rapist can be seen righteous in the eyes of the Lord and have a new nature and a pure heart. God's ways are certainly higher than any human's ways!

It is now our choice to yield to the Spirit of God or to our old nature, which is often referred to as the flesh in the Bible. We didn't have a choice before salvation. We only had the one nature. We didn't have the power to say no to that old, carnal (fleshly/worldly) nature; however, now, we can overcome that old nature, and we can choose to purify our hearts. "For to be carnally minded is death; but to be spiritually minded is life and peace. Because the carnal mind is enmity against God: for it is not subject to the law of God, neither indeed can be. So then they that are in the flesh cannot please God. But ye are not in the flesh, but in the Spirit, if so be that the Spirit of God dwell in you. Now if any man have not the Spirit of Christ, he is none of his. And if Christ be in you, the body is dead because of sin; but the Spirit is life because of righteousness. But if the Spirit of him that raised up Jesus from the dead dwell in you, he that raised up Christ from the dead shall also quicken your mortal bodies by his Spirit that dwelleth in you. Therefore, brethren, we are debtors, not to the flesh, to live after the flesh. For if ye live after the flesh, ye shall die: but if ye through the Spirit do mortify the deeds of the body, ye shall live. For as many as are led by the Spirit of God, they are the sons of God." (Romans 8:6-14)

Now, we can have a pure heart. You may then ask, how do I get a clean heart? If my heart is desperately wicked, isn't it true that I have no chance to see God? The previous verses told us that we now have power to have an unpolluted heart, and we have a debt to our God to have that pure heart.

The first way that anyone can have a clean heart is to realize that it is not clean—we must recognize our sinfulness. This is the first beatitude—that attitude that produces true happiness—to be poor in spirit. We must recognize "I'm not pure" before we will ever be pure in heart. Again, we can't see God without a pure heart, and we can't get saved unless we realize that we are sinners and need a Savior, so it is salvation that opens this door of purity of heart.

Once I realize that I am not pure, I must come to the One who can make my heart pure: God. It is not just that initial salvation, but it is a continuing in the Word of God that keeps the heart clean—a reliance on who God is and what God had done and will do in, through, and for us. "Wherewithal shall a young man cleanse his way? by taking heed thereto according to thy word." (Psalm 119:9)

To take heed is not to occasionally read the Word of God, but it is to hedge about (as with thorns), to guard, to attend to, to be circumspect "according to thy word." This is saying guard your life and live by the rule of the Word of God. Circumspect means cautious; watchful on all sides; examining carefully all the circumstances that may affect a determination.

Purity is not about the outside. It is about the heart. God is always considering the heart. "Every way of a man is right in his own eyes: but the LORD pondereth the hearts." (Proverbs 21:2) In fact, it is the heart that He is talking about with all these beatitudes. They are heart attitudes that reflect themselves in action. While others may only see the outside, God is focused on the heart, and what is in the heart will show itself on the outside.

Recognizing that we are impure, then going to God daily to cleanse us and keep us clean is a good start. However, even being in the Word every day, our hearts can sneakily start to reign and before we know it, we'll be back to "I think, I want, I feel" even while reading and studying the Word of God.

How, then, do we remain pure in heart?

God does the work. "Being confident of this very thing, that he which hath begun a good work in you will perform it until the day of Jesus Christ:" (Philippians 1:6)

In God's unmatchable love, He draws us back to Himself. If we are in the Word of God, He will use His Words to speak to our Spirit and thoughts so that the heart may be turned back to Him. "For the Word of God is quick, and powerful, and sharper than any twoedged sword, piercing even to the dividing asunder of soul and spirit, and of the joints and marrow, and is a discerner of the thoughts and intents of the heart." (Hebrews 4:12)

Notice the words of strength and power indicated for the Word of God—quick, which means alive; powerful—full of power; sharper than any two-edged sword. Then we see that the Word of God pierces to the dividing asunder of soul and spirit. Dividing asunder means separation. What does the Word separate? The soul and spirit aka what I think, feel, and want and what God thinks, feels, and wants.

That is the first way that God attempts to draw us back to Himself once we have started to shift back into the comfort of "I." Of course, we need to be paying attention. If that doesn't work, God then begins to use situations to draw us back to Him, which is something that needs done on a regular basis, even if we are going in the right way. The Bible speaks of the refinery process.

I was not at all familiar with this concept before reading my Bible and studying some things out. For precious metals to be at their purest forms, they are put to the fire to remove all the impurities from them. Once that happens, the metal, such as gold or silver, is shinier and more glorious. The Bible refers to this process for the Christian as well.

"For thou, O God, hast proved us: thou hast tried us, as silver is tried." (Psalm 66:10) "Behold, I have refined thee, but not with silver; I have chosen thee in the furnace of affliction." (Isaiah 48:10)

Refining is part of the Christian life to keep us pure, to continually grow us to be more like Christ. Of course, this may go against our natural way of thinking. We might think that if I follow God and do what is right that nothing bad should happen to me and that I shouldn't have to go through affliction. Many "so-called" Christians teach this. However, it is not what the Word of God teaches.

Before God went silent for 400 years at the end of the writing of the Old Testament, He spoke through the prophet Zechariah: "And it shall come to pass, that in all the land, saith the LORD, two parts therein shall be cut off and die; but the third shall be left therein. And I will bring the third part through the fire, and will refine them as silver is refined, and will try them as gold is tried: they shall call on my name, and I will hear them: I will say, It is my people: and they shall say, The LORD is my God." (Zechariah 13:8-9) He prophesied of Jesus' death and of the scattering of the saints in the verses before. Then we see that most people will not have hearts that are right toward God—two thirds, the Bible tells us—and will be cut off and die. Yet, a remnant, the one third left, will be tried/refined as silver/gold is refined. Why? They and we will call out to God, will see God, and will be known as the children of God.

No matter if we are in bad circumstances because of our sin, somebody else's sin, or God is just trying to get our attention or move us along, as Christians, we should call on the Lord. We should draw close to Him, and we will grow from the situation. It is part of the reason that we go through hard times as we are told in 1 Peter: "That the trial of your faith, being much more precious than of gold that perisheth, though it be tried with fire, might be found unto praise and honour and glory at the appearing of Jesus Christ:" (1 Peter 1:7)

If we are stubborn and still don't turn to the Lord and allow our hearts to be cleaned up, we will find ourselves in harsher situations, eventually (though with much mercy, grace, and longsuffering) leading to an end of life on earth. God will bring the Christian home who chooses not to heed to His rule. He takes us home, so that we can no longer tarnish His name or hurt ourselves and others.

Of course, this is not what He desires most. He does want to be with us, but He would rather prefer that each of us desires to please Him and chooses to be about His business while we have time on earth. He wants us to have a pure heart so that we can see Him with the purpose that we can show others who He is.

In the Book of James, we are instructed and admonished, "But He giveth more grace. Wherefore He saith, God resisteth the proud, but giveth grace unto the humble. Submit yourselves therefore to God. Resist the devil, and he will flee from you. Draw nigh to God, and He will draw nigh to you. Cleanse your hands, ye sinners; and purify your hearts, ye double minded. Be afflicted, and mourn, and weep: let your laughter be turned to mourning, and your joy to heaviness. Humble yourselves in the sight of the Lord, and He shall lift you up." (James 4:6-10)

God is love. He is not looking to punish us but bless us. It is always His desire to give grace to His children more than punish them. However, it is on us. If through the grace, as God shows us that we are having impure thoughts, motives, or desires, we are prideful and ignore those pleas to turn back to Him, we cannot say how much longer He will deal as such with us. As a principle in RU says "We lose our power to choose when we give into temptation. The consequences are inevitable, incalculable, and up to God."

Purity starts from within not without. In our search for purity, we must be sure not to focus on the outside—the actions, though our actions are a window to the heart. "Beware of false prophets, which come to you in sheep's clothing, but inwardly they are ravening wolves. Ye shall know them by their fruits. Do men gather grapes of thorns, or figs of thistles? Even so every good tree bringeth forth good fruit; but a corrupt tree bringeth forth evil fruit. A good tree cannot bring forth evil fruit, neither can a corrupt tree bring forth good fruit." (Matthew 7:15-18) Without the internal being changed, external purity will not last, and our fruit will tell of what is truly in our hearts.

Purity doesn't happen without fire and pruning like those precious metals or plants. When God shows us something is impure, we need to put effort into getting it out of our lives—put that thing off, as we talked about in Chapter four and put on something that God would be pleased with. Don't run away from those things that make us stronger and wiser—even the afflicting times in our lives. They are meant to squeeze us and make it clear what is inside. Then they are to direct us to our loving heavenly Father so that we can trust Him, acknowledge Him in all of our ways and He will direct our paths. (Proverbs 3:5-7)

The corruption of the world doesn't bring happiness. Although it is the "norm," and many will claim happiness and freedom, we must ask ourselves does their fruit show happiness and freedom? How many people feel they NEED to drink, get high, punch somebody, start a new relationship, spend money...etc., every day because the God-sized hole in their life isn't filled?

It's time to let go of all the poison that we've been told isn't so bad. Let go of the t.v. shows, the movies, the music, the friends, the books, the substances...etc., that hold you back from having a pure heart to see God—that are holding you back from true happiness.

Do you want to see God? Do you want to know who He is? Do you want Him in your life? Do you want Him in your ministry? Would you like to see Him work in your family? "Blessed are the pure in heart: for they shall see God." (Matthew 5:8)

How to have a pure heart:

1)   **Remain.** Continue in the Word of God. Set a daily time of Bible reading and prayer, so that God can reveal your heart to you, and you can commune with Him.

- "All scripture is given by inspiration of God, and is profitable for doctrine, for reproof, for correction, for instruction in righteousness: That the man of God may be perfect, throughly furnished unto all good works." (2 Timothy 3:16-17)
- "ALEPH. Blessed are the undefiled in the way, who walk in the law of the LORD. Blessed are they that keep his testimonies, and that seek him with the whole heart. They also do no iniquity: they walk in his ways. Thou hast commanded us to keep thy precepts diligently. O that my ways were directed to keep thy statutes! Then shall I not be ashamed, when I have respect unto all thy commandments." (Psalm 119:1-6)

2)   **Repent.** Agree with God, always. Check your thoughts, feelings, and desires and make sure that they align with the Word of God. When they don't, remember that it is He who is right and agree with Him.

- "There is a way which seemeth right unto a man, but the end thereof are the ways of death." (Proverbs 14:12)
- "But if we walk in the light, as he is in the light, we have fellowship one with another, and the blood of Jesus Christ his Son cleanseth us from all sin. If we say that we have no sin, we deceive ourselves, and the truth is not in us. If we confess our sins, he is faithful and just to forgive us our sins, and to cleanse us from all unrighteousness." (1 John 1:7-9)

3)   **Remember.** Remember God. Remember what He has done for you. Remember His love. Remember His mercy. Remember who you were before you met Him. Remember how good He has been to you since. Remember!

- "Because thy lovingkindness is better than life, my lips shall praise thee. Thus will I bless thee while I live: I will lift up my hands in thy name. My soul shall be satisfied as with marrow and fatness; and my mouth shall praise thee with joyful lips: When I remember thee upon my bed, and meditate on thee in the night watches. Because thou hast been my help, therefore in the shadow of thy wings will I rejoice. My soul followeth hard after thee: thy right hand upholdeth me. But those that seek my soul, to destroy it, shall go into the lower parts of the earth." (Psalm 63:3-9)
- "And their sins and iniquities will I remember no more" – God (Hebrews 10:17)

4)   **Repeat.** Go back and do 1–3 repeatedly. Continue in the ways of the Lord that you might have a clean heart to see God and know true happiness.

- "Then said Jesus to those Jews which believed on him, If ye continue in my word, then are ye my disciples indeed; And ye shall know the truth, and the truth shall make you free." (John 8:31-32)

- "Confirming the souls of the disciples, and exhorting them to continue in the faith, and that we must through much tribulation enter into the kingdom of God." (Acts 14:22)
- "Let brotherly love continue." (Hebrews 13:1)
- "As the Father hath loved me, so have I loved you: continue ye in my love." (John 15:9)
- "Continue in prayer, and watch in the same with thanksgiving;" (Colossians 4:2)

"I would sooner be holy than happy if the two things could be divorced. Were it possible for a man always to sorrow and yet to be pure, I would choose the sorrow if I might win the purity, for to be free from the power of sin, to be made to love holiness, is true happiness." - Charles Spurgeon

~ 6 ~

PART II: BIBLICAL EXAMPLE

Pure in Heart—Hananiah, Mishael, Azariah and the Fiery Furnace

Sixteen years after Daniel chapter two when Nebuchadnezzar proclaims Daniel's God to be God of gods because Daniel could reveal and interpret a dream, Nebuchadnezzar built a 90-foot golden statue of himself and gathered the people together to worship it. His proclamation was that if any worshipped not the statue, they would be thrown into a fiery furnace.

Daniel had three loyal friends who were at this great spectacle that the king had set up. Hananiah, Mishael, and Azariah did not bow to the statue that day, and some Chaldeans (native Babylonians) went to the king to report the Hebrew men for refusing to obey the king's command.

King Nebuchadnezzar had the three men brought to him and repeated his command and the terrible consequences for anyone who would go against that order—be thrown into the fire. "Now if ye be ready that at what time ye hear the sound of the cornet, flute, harp, sackbut, psaltery, and dulcimer, and all kinds of musick, ye fall down and worship the image which I have made; well: but if ye worship not, ye shall be cast the same hour into the midst of a burning fiery furnace; and who is that God that shall deliver you out of my hands?" (Daniel 3:15) The king was so full of himself that he was willing to do the whole thing over just so Hananiah, Mishael, and Azariah could bow down to his idol. Nebuchadnezzar's heart was full of pride and there was no remembrance of what God had done for him as he even defies God and challenges Him: "...and who is that God that shall deliver you out of my hands?"

Wicked hearts are easily seen. The Chaldeans were laying in wait to catch the Hebrews in something because of their jealousy, their hearts impure with selfishness, ambition, and envy stirring them. The king's heart was openly rebellious against the God of gods, filled with pride, selfishness, haughtiness and ill-will, willing to send some of God's people into the fire.

We also see the pure hearts easily noticeable among the rest. There they were in a scary, life-threatening situation. It would've been easy for their hearts to embrace fear, self-preservation, and hopelessness. However, we see in their response that their hearts were filled with God: "Shadrach, Meshach, and Abednego, answered and said to the king, O Nebuchadnezzar, we are not careful to answer thee in this matter. If it be so, our God whom we serve is able to deliver us from the burning fiery furnace, and he will deliver us out of thine hand, O king. But if not, be it known unto thee, O king, that we will not serve thy gods, nor worship the golden image which thou hast set up." (Daniel 3:16-18)

What amazing purity of heart which led to them putting their faith in action! Their response was that God was able to deliver them, but even if He didn't, they chose Him over worshipping the statue of Nebuchadnezzar or any of their gods.

What was the outcome of those men who had pure hearts toward God? "Then was Nebuchadnezzar full of fury, and the form of his visage was changed against Shadrach, Meshach, and Abednego: therefore he spake, and commanded that they should heat the furnace one seven times more than it was wont to be heated. And he commanded the most mighty men that were in his army to bind Shadrach, Meshach, and Abednego, and to cast them into the burning fiery furnace. Then these men were bound in their coats, their hosen, and their hats, and their other garments, and were cast into the midst of the burning fiery furnace." (Daniel 3:19-21)

They were thrown into an extremely hot fiery furnace!

That doesn't seem like the response to a pure heart that we would expect. Yet, was it any different for the One with the purest heart ever? No. Jesus, who was tempted in all ways like us, yet without sin, was murdered even though He had a pure heart toward God. It was some of the same impure hearts that hung him on a tree, and so we see that when Hannaniah, Mishael, and Azariah (aka Shadrach, Meshach and Abednego) were in that fire, Jesus was in there with them. "Blessed are the pure in heart: for they shall see God." (Matthew 5:8)

However, before we see them with Jesus in the fire, we see that those who threw the three pure-hearted Hebrew men into the fire got burned by the fire and died. They had a chance to stand for God there. They had a chance to get rid of the impurities of self and fear there, yet, they obeyed the king, and it was not a good thing for them to face God.

Nebuchadezzar saw his men die by the flame and as he looked in the fire he was amazed as he saw Jesus in the midst of the fire with Hananiah, Mishael, and Azariah, and the three men weren't hurt by the fire. "Then Nebuchadnezzar the king was astonied, and rose up in haste, and spake, and said unto his counsellors, Did not we cast three men bound into the midst of the fire? They answered and said unto the king, True, O king. He answered and said, Lo, I see four men loose, walking in the midst of the fire, and they have no hurt; and the form of the fourth is like the Son of God." (Daniel 3:24-25)

When the pure in heart have to deal with tough situations and God shows up, people also see God because of them—because of we who will give our whole hearts to the Savior. It wasn't just the king who saw those men untouched by the fire, it was all that was in attendance, and there Nebuchadnezzar praised God and made a new decree that if anyone spoke against those Hebrew men's God, they would be killed "because there is no other God that can deliver after this sort." (Daniel 3:29b)

What became of those men who chose to have their hearts pure before God? They were promoted again. God exalted them. "He that loveth pureness of heart, for the grace of his lips the king shall be his friend." (Proverbs 22:11) Even though they had defied the king, God showed up for those who gave their whole hearts to Him, which turned the heart of the king toward them.

Thankfully we are not under such tyranny as were those Hebrew men. However, it is getting harder and harder to exalt the name of God, to continue in a pure heart, and to live for God without some-one attempting to tear you down. It is important that we learn from these men and continue developing a pure heart—getting rid of all things that are defiled from our heart (thoughts, feelings, desires) and replacing them with things that are pure, lovely and of good report—the Word of God, the character of God, the promises of God and remember the deeds of God. It may just be that as people see you stand up for God, make it through a tough situation, they may see God because you have seen God. Amen!

It's true that one day we will all see God as He is and will bow down and worship Him. "For it is written, As I live, saith the Lord, every knee shall bow to me, and every tongue shall confess to God. So then every one of us shall give account of himself to God." (Romans 14:11-12) However, when we see Him while on earth, we not only see Him in eternity, like Shadrach, Meshach and Abednego, we can see Him work miraculously in our daily lives. Let's just re-member that they had to go through the fire in order to see God.

The Bible tells us that all people will get a chance of purity of heart. "For the grace of God that bringeth salvation hath appeared to all men, Teaching us that, denying ungodliness and worldly lusts, we should live soberly, righteously, and godly, in this present world; Looking for that blessed hope, and the glorious appearing of the great God and our Saviour Jesus Christ; Who gave himself for us, that he might redeem us from all iniquity, and purify unto himself a peculiar people, zealous of good works." (Titus 2:11-14)

The grace of God has appeared to all men, meaning all of humanity. This grace—this salvation teaches us to live with a pure heart and always look toward Jesus who loves us and died for us. Why do we live with a pure heart? Because others are watching and while we are saved and going to heaven, it might just be our pure hearts and responses to things in the world that helps others see their need for Jesus too.

Not only will it bring happiness to us as we live without those things that bring death, it may bring happiness to others.

Consider some people who the grace of God appeared to—they saw God yet refused to glorify Him as God. What was their end? What will it be like when they face God at the judgment? What about yourself? What will it be like when you face God at the judgment? What if it came today? How about your daily life—do you see God working in your thoughts, in your feelings, and in your desires? Have you seen Him at work in your situations?

~ 6 ~

PART III: PERSONAL EXAMPLE

I love music. I have always loved music, but music is one of those things that preferences matter in. Music choice has a lot to do with what I think, what I feel, and what I desire.

I will never forget the day that God showed me something about the music that I had listened to all of my life. About three weeks after dedicating my life to the Lord, continuing in Bible study and church attendance, I did what was custom for me: After worship service Sunday morning, I would go home, turn on my music, crank it up, and clean my house.

That day, I did just that, and that day the words sounded differently. In fact, it hurt my heart to hear such words blasting through my speakers. It was like I was hearing that song that I had listened to countless times for the very first time. God had showed me the impurity of my music.

Because I could hear the music in a different way, it wasn't hard for me to gather up all my cds and throw them away. I felt bad for having my children listen to such garbage. Now, I know that some of the music that I choose to listen to today, some Christians would describe as garbage as well, but God has not told me that.

As we learned in this chapter, the heart is deceitful and wicked. Without the Word of God, I never would've changed my mind on music. He had to show me the impurities and then I had to step out in faith and agree with Him that I was wrong.

As Christians, we like to believe that we are often pure in heart, but I have found that a lot of the time, my heart is mixed with my feelings, thoughts, and desires and therefore is not pure. Music is one of the hardest things to speak on because it is so divided among Christians and that is because it is based on preference. I don't like to give advice on music for that reason. I'd rather let God convict a person of their music choice, the way that He did with me, than turn a person away from Jesus because of such a thing. "Let us not therefore judge one another any more: but judge this rather, that no man put a stumblingblock or an occasion to fall in his brother's way." (Romans 14:13)

Unfortunately, purity of heart, as one might think in themselves, can be just the opposite.

Recently, God has shown me that an area that I thought I was pure in heart in, in reality, I was not. I have always given to my local church since I got right with the Lord. It just felt natural. I didn't have money to give when I first got in, so I gave of my time and energy. Soon God began to show me that I have talents, and I started to give my talents to the local church. For the last three years I have been able to give money to the church, and that felt good to me, especially since my time and talents were taken up in other places.

It is good to give. God tells us that. However, our motive is more important than what or how much we give. Just recently I realized that my motive wasn't all about God. Shocking! I know. Part of it was about me. It FELT good to give, and I gave from my abundance. Notice, when I had abundant time, I gave of my time. When I had extra money, I gave of my money, but time was limited so I didn't give much of it.

When I tell you that this chapter has been convicting to me, it is an understatement. Truly considering my thoughts, feelings, and desires to be pure, I have come up short; however, I have become aware, and it is changing my thoughts. Praise the Lord!

Money has been tight lately and would you believe that I began to pull back my tithes from the local church? I did. I stopped trusting God and began to lean on my own understanding. I did this for months before God made it clear to me what I was doing. I thought I was doing what was best for my family, making sure there was food in the house and the bills were paid. Those things are important—vital, even. Yet, all those things were still a struggle. Money remained tight.

Since God opened my eyes, I decided the very next pay I was going to give to God first as I had done previously. I would trust Him. I gave of those moneys that I had promised to missions and to my local church and had very little to buy groceries and pay my rent. The very next day, God began sending groceries my way—no lie! That Monday extra food came, and then Wednesday even more food came, and wouldn't you know it, Friday another set of groceries was given to me and my family.

I can't explain this. It's God. We didn't struggle this past week because I surrendered my money to Him first. One might think how this has to do with being pure in heart. It took me letting go of my thoughts, feelings, and desires and replacing them with God's thoughts, feelings, and desires so that I could give to Him first. That is not a natural thing. I needed that purity of heart to trust God and then to walk by faith, giving to eternal matters before giving to physical needs.

I've learned something about myself these past three months, and it has opened my eyes to consider what other ways I am not pure in heart so that God's blessing can be in my life and in all that I do. "Every man according as he purposeth in his heart, so let him give; not grudgingly, or of necessity: for God loveth a cheerful giver." (2 Corinthians 9:7)

Giving is important, but this chapter isn't about giving necessarily. It is about the heart. It is about purity of heart. The heart is where God looks, and it is our duty to focus our hearts, protect our hearts, and lead our hearts because out of it are the issues of life (Proverbs 4:23). The word purposeth means to choose for oneself before another; to prefer. Purity is all about preference. Do we prefer God and His way, or do we prefer our own way or the way of the world?

"Blessed are the pure in heart: for they shall see God." (Matthew 5:8) I saw God show up in a big way this past week. When was the last time you saw God do something in your life?

~ 6 ~

PART IV: GO DEEPER

1. What does pure mean?

____

____

2. What does the Bible refer to when it uses the word heart?

____

____

3. Give your own definition of what it means to be pure in heart.

____

____

____

4. What are our hearts if left to themselves according to Jeremiah 17:9?

____

____

5. The Word of God says "Keep thy heart with all diligence; for out of it are the issues of life." (Proverbs 4:23)

a. Using a Bible dictionary, what does the word keep mean?

____

____

b. Why are we told to keep our hearts?

____

____

6. How can we have a clean heart/path, according to Psalm 119:9 and 119:11?

----

7. You may think that you have come too far, and a pure heart is out of your reach because you have filled your heart with too much of the world or your self. David, as king, committed sin. He took another man's wife for a night. The woman got pregnant, so he tried to cover up the sin by having her husband lie with her; however Uriah was a good man who would not take pleasure at wartime but remained with David to protect him. David's sin got darker as he had Uriah sent to the front of the battlefield where he knew he wouldn't make it. He tried to make everything look good by marrying the widow Bathsheba who was pregnant with his child. Nobody knew what had happened. David, even, got so far away from God that he continued judging the people without repentance for months. Yet, when David was confronted by the prophet Nathan, he turns his heart from himself to God and repents. Read 2 Samuel 11 and 12 for this account.

a. David wrote Psalm 51 after that confrontation. He mentions being clean/pure several times in this Psalm. Read it. Study it. Take notes about it. Recall Psalm 51 when God shows you something that you have done against Him and be sure that you have repented—turned from that thing and to Him.

8. According to the following verses, what is more important, our outside appearance (what we look like, do and say) or our internal motivations (what we think, feel and desire—our heart)?

- "But the LORD said unto Samuel, Look not on his countenance, or on the height of his stature; because I have refused him: for the LORD seeth not as man seeth; for man looketh on the outward appearance, but the LORD looketh on the heart." (1 Samuel 16:7)

The next king of Israel was being chosen. It was a great task that Samuel was sent to do. God sent Samuel to the house of Jesse where Samuel assumed that the eldest son was the one that he was sent for, however we see God's response in 1 Samuel 16:7: "...for the LORD seeth not as man seeth; for man looketh on the outward appearance, but the LORD looketh on the heart."

Samuel called the next and the next, a total of seven of Jesse's children, but none of them were chosen. Finally, Samuel asked Jesse if all of his sons were there, and it was found that one son remained, the youngest who was ruddy and the keeper of their sheep, David.

According to outside appearances, even David's dad didn't think David would be chosen as king. Perhaps for you, you have looked at your outside appearance, your level of schooling, your popularity or lack in some way and think that there is no way that God could use you, but God wasn't after someone who looked the right way or said all the right things. He was looking for someone who had a heart toward Him and He chose David.

Yes, the same David who we studied about who had that great sin and wrote that great psalm of repentance. He is said to have a heart after God's own heart: "And when he had removed him, he raised up unto them David to be their king; to whom also he gave testimony, and said, I have found David the son of Jesse, a man after mine own heart, which shall fulfil all my will." (Acts 13:22)

He wasn't perfect. His heart had wandered at times and became polluted with himself and things of the world, but David never let it remain corrupt. When he saw that he was wrong, he repented, turned back to God and started on the path that God had for him, even being willing to take the consequences of his behavior while away from God. He got back to the place where he had a pure heart toward God that what God thought, felt, and wanted was more important than what David thought, felt, and wanted.

That is what God wants from us. In fact, let's look at what Jesus says about some other people that were called into the service of God.

- "Woe unto you, scribes and Pharisees, hypocrites! for ye make clean the outside of the cup and of the platter, but within they are full of extortion and excess. 26Thou blind Pharisee, cleanse first that which is within the cup and platter, that the outside of them may be clean also. 27Woe unto you, scribes and Pharisees, hypocrites! for ye are like unto whited sepulchres, which indeed appear beautiful outward, but are within full of dead men's bones, and of all uncleanness. 28Even so ye also outwardly appear righteous unto men, but within ye are full of hypocrisy and iniquity." (Matthew 23:25-28)

____

____

____

Jesus is talking to the religious leaders of that day (Scribes and Pharisees).

i. What three ways does Jesus describe them? (v. 25, 26, 27)

____

____

____

ii. What is a hypocrite?

____

____

iii. Why does Jesus call these leaders hypocrites? (v. 25)

____

____

____

iv. Jesus tells them, and us, that if we cleanse what first, the outside will be clean? (v. 26)

____

v. Based on what we learned in this chapter, what do you think this means? How does it apply to your life?

\---

\---

\---

\---

\---

vi. What is the comparison made in verse 27? You may have to look up the word sepulchre.

\---

\---

\---

\---

\---

vii. How can that comparison apply to our hearts/lives as we walk in service to the Lord or with lip service to the Lord and our hearts are mixed with a lot of self, pride, fear...etc.?

\---

\---

\---

\---

\---

9. What are some steps that we can take to have a pure heart, as discussed in this chapter?

\---

\---

\---

\---

10. Can you think of some things that you need to start doing today that will help you have a pure heart? Write them down and take inventory regularly of what is going on in your heart. We must put in effort, attention, and time daily to grow.

\---

\---

---

11. What is your greatest takeaway(s) from this chapter on being pure in heart? Has anything surprised you?

---

12. If you took inventory of your heart today, would you say that it is pure? Why? If not, what impurities remain? Look up some Scriptures about those things that are prevalent in your thoughts, feelings, and desires and align them with what God thinks, feels, and desires.

~ 7 ~

BLESSED ARE THE PEACEMAKERS

Part I—INSIGHT: Gaining Knowledge

Blessed are the peacemakers: for they shall be called the children of God. (Matthew 5:9)

I believe that besides love and happiness, peace is the most sought after treasure in our world today. How would you define peace? It is generally defined as freedom from disturbance; tranquility or a state or period in which there is no war, or a war has ended. A peacemaker is generally defined to be one who brings about peace (freedom from disturbance; tranquility or a state/period with no conflict), especially by reconciling adversaries.

Biblically, peace is more than just the absence of things that stir us up. It is safety. It comes from the Hebrew word shalom which means to be complete or to live well. There are four main categories of this Hebrew word "peace": wholeness of health or body; right relationships; prosperity and success; and a greeting or farewell to wish blessing to another person. When a Hebrew used "shalom" they meant "God's highest good for you." In RU, we define peace as being safe in mind, body, and spirit. I think that definition covers the Hebrew word shalom.

There are many people who are all about wholeness in the body. They study and teach how one can eat well and exercise to have great health. Others are conscious of the mind and value education and brain exercises to keep the mind healthy. Some focus on the mental health of individuals to bring about complete health. There are even some who will combine such studies and teach and collaborate with others to develop the areas of body and mind in hopes to bring happiness and peace to their lives.

Some people focus on the spirit—not the Spirit of God—but the human spirit. They study eastern meditation and yoga and believe that such activities will bring peace and happiness.

Yet, all three groups of people fail to bring true peace to the lives of those that they invest in; therefore, their happiness, if it comes at all, is short-lived. All three areas of study and service miss the main thing: God is the one who brings peace.

As the Bible prophesied of the coming Messiah in Isaiah 9:6, we were told that His name would be the Prince of Peace: "For unto us a child is born, unto us a son is given: and the government shall be upon his shoulder: and his name shall be called Wonderful, Counsellor, The mighty God, The everlasting Father, The Prince of Peace." (Isaiah 9:6)

There is only one way to be safe in mind, body, and spirit and that is through our Lord, Jesus Christ. God is the God of peace. "Now the God of peace, that brought again from the dead our Lord Jesus, that great shepherd of the sheep, through the blood of the everlasting covenant," (Hebrews 13:20) "Now the Lord of peace himself give you peace always by all means. The Lord be with you all." (2 Thessalonians 3:16)

If the definition of peace is deeper than an absence of conflict, then peacemaker must be deeper than one who pacifies conflict.

A peacemaker is one who will do their best to remove conflict from their own life and others. They will promote kindness and reconciliation between disputing parties. However, a peacemaker understands that the enemy of peace is not disagreement. The enemy of peace is not even conflict. The enemy of peace is sin.

The God of peace created everything in peace. The angels and humanity were at peace with God. Angels were at peace with other angels and Adam was at peace with Eve. Even the animals were at peace with each other. "And God saw every thing that he had made, and, behold, it was very good. And the evening and the morning were the sixth day." (Genesis 1:31)

Then entered pride and a rebellious thought against God, which, with free will, led to war between God and Satan and 1/3 of the angels. "How art thou fallen from heaven, O Lucifer, son of the morning! how art thou cut down to the ground, which didst weaken the nations! For thou hast said in thine heart, I will ascend into heaven, I will exalt my throne above the stars of God: I will sit also upon the mount of the congregation, in the sides of the north: I will ascend above the heights of the clouds; I will be like the most High. Yet thou shalt be brought down to hell, to the sides of the pit. (Isaiah 14:12-15) (Ezekiel 28; Revelation 12:4).

Satan was not satisfied with only taking those angels to his damnation; he set his eyes on God's precious creation, mankind, whom He authorized to have authority over every other creation in the earth and to be the giver of the Gospel and manifestation of the grace of God. "What is man, that thou art mindful of him? or the son of man, that thou visitest him? Thou madest him a little lower than the angels; thou crownedst him with glory and honour, and didst set him over the works of thy hands:" (Hebrews 2:6-7)

All things changed on earth once sin entered the world, outside the heavens. "But of the tree of the knowledge of good and evil, thou shalt not eat of it: for in the day that thou eatest thereof thou shalt surely die." (Genesis 2:17) "And the serpent said unto the woman, Ye shall not surely die: For God doth know that in the day ye eat thereof, then your eyes shall be opened, and ye shall be as gods, knowing good and evil. And when the woman saw that the tree was good for food, and that it was pleasant to the eyes, and a tree to be desired to make one wise, she took of the fruit thereof, and did eat, and gave also unto her husband with her; and he did eat. And the eyes of them both were opened, and they knew that they were naked; and they sewed fig leaves together, and made themselves aprons." (Genesis 3:4-7) The world has known evil since then.

Adam and Eve had a new friction, and every one of their children as well as their offspring forever would be, and are, born sinners. Animals no longer lived in peace with one another. Even the plants have a struggle to live in the earth. With sin came dire consequences—death, just as God said there would be.

Death means separation. Satan and the angels that followed him are separated from God and know no peace therefore bring no peace. Every human is born separated from God. It is not until we make a personal decision to believe in Jesus as Savior that we can be at peace with God again. That restoration to the God of peace brings us peace—wholeness; safety in mind, spirit, and body. Peace brings happiness. "Therefore being justified by faith, we have peace with God through our Lord Jesus Christ: By whom also we have access by faith into this grace wherein we stand, and rejoice in hope of the glory of God." (Romans 5:1-2)

Sin, the enemy of peace, must be destroyed in order to bring peace again, and at salvation indwelling sin, the power of sin in our lives, is destroyed. "Know ye not, that so many of us as were baptized into Jesus Christ were baptized into his death? Therefore we are buried with him by baptism into death: that like as Christ was raised up from the dead by the glory of the Father, even so we also should walk in newness of life. For if we have been planted together in the likeness of his death, we shall be also in the likeness of his resurrection: Knowing this, that our old man is crucified with him, that the body of sin might be destroyed, that henceforth we should not serve sin. For he that is dead is freed from sin." (Romans 6:3-8) "Know ye not, that to whom ye yield yourselves servants to obey, his servants ye are to whom ye obey; whether of sin unto death, or of obedience unto righteousness? But God be thanked, that ye were the servants of sin, but ye have obeyed from the heart that form of doctrine which was delivered you. Being then made free from sin, ye became the servants of righteousness." (Romans 6:16-18)

Without sin, we can know peace, and because we know peace, we can be peacemakers. Understanding peace makes us better understand what a peacemaker that God is talking about in Matthew 5 expresses—This special group of people that will be known as the children of God.

The Word of God tells us that wisdom from above is first pure, then peaceable, which brings the fruit of righteousness and peace in others' lives. "But the wisdom that is from above is first pure, then peaceable, gentle, and easy to be intreated, full of mercy and good fruits, without partiality, and without hypocrisy. And the fruit of righteousness is sown in peace of them that make peace." (James 3:17-18)

By our definition of peace and the above verse, we can say that a peacemaker is one who restores people to the peace of God which brings peace in all areas of life. Surprisingly a peacemaker is not without conflict. In fact, we find that if we are going to be a peacemaker, we will often find ourselves in conflict with others.

Why? People aren't a big fan of the truth anymore. People don't want purity and righteousness in their lives. They do; but they aren't willing to give up what it costs to get it. They prefer their sin. "And this is the condemnation, that light is come into the world, and men loved darkness rather than light, because their deeds were evil. For every one that doeth evil hateth the light, neither cometh to the light, lest his deeds should be reproved." (John 3:19-20)

It takes the peacemaker to first live a pure, peaceable life in God around others and then to teach the truth of God so that when the Holy Spirit visits them, they will be ready to say yes. "Dearly beloved, I beseech you as strangers and pilgrims, abstain from fleshly lusts, which war against the soul; Having your conversation honest among the Gentiles: that, whereas they speak against you as evildoers, they may by your good works, which they shall behold, glorify God in the day of visitation." (1 Peter 2:11-12)

Many confuse peacemaking with peacekeeping. A peacekeeper is one who either avoids conflict or compromises morals and values for the return of a false peace. Peacekeepers will not be called the children of God because they don't stand with God. They are blown every which way trying to "keep the peace" when they should be firm with the Truth in order to bring true peace.

Our peace came at a great cost. It was by great pain, persecution, and perseverance that peace can be possible our world. Our Savior willingly faced persecution and great pain to the point of death out of love and perseverance to bring us peace—to give us the freedom from sin that shackles us and brings war within ourselves, toward others, and toward our God. "But he was wounded for our transgressions, he was bruised for our iniquities: the chastisement of our peace was upon him; and with his stripes we are healed." (Isaiah 53:5)

There is no greater happiness than to be free from sin—the control of sin. That is peace—absolute safety in mind, body, and spirit. No matter what happens, it is well with my soul. "...to the counsellors of peace is joy." (Proverbs 12:20b)

It's true that shortly after the beginning of time, we've seen the opposite of peace be prevalent. From the first person born on earth, Cain, to the current war between Russia and Ukraine and every other battle within and without, it has been conflict after conflict after conflict.

Peace treaties have been signed. People have been jailed and "rehabilitated." Drugs and coping methods have been distributed like candy, yet war still reigns. Why? Our world is full of peace-keepers not peacemakers. Sin is still the enemy of peace. Sin must be destroyed in each person's life in order for peace to be prevalent. So, one person at a time, let's take the message of peace to the world. Let's be peacemakers! In doing so we will see happiness spread like a rainbow after the rain of a sun-shiny day.

So, how can we be peacemakers instead of peacekeepers?

1)   **Be reconciled to God**. The first thing is to be born again. We need the Spirit and nature of God in order to be reconciled to God so that sin doesn't have rule over us and so that we desire to see true peace in others. "Therefore if any man be in Christ, he is a new creature: old things are passed away; behold, all things are become new. And all things are of God, who hath reconciled us to himself by Jesus Christ, and hath given to us the ministry of reconciliation; To wit, that God was in Christ, reconciling the world unto himself, not imputing their trespasses unto them; and hath committed unto us the word of reconciliation. Now then we are ambassadors for Christ, as though God did beseech you by us: we pray you in Christ's stead, be ye reconciled to God. For he hath made him to be sin for us, who knew no sin; that we might be made the righteousness of God in him." (2 Corinthians 5:17-21)

2)   **Be in fellowship with God**. Once we are saved, we have the ability and a desire to be a peacemaker; however, we must also keep short accounts with God in order to remain in the power of Christ and to continue to have the desire to see others come to Him. "For it pleased the Father that in him should all fulness dwell; And, having made peace through the blood of his cross, by him to reconcile all things unto himself; by him, I say, whether they be things in earth, or things in heaven. And you, that were sometime alienated and enemies in your mind by wicked works, yet now hath he reconciled In the body of his flesh through death, to present you holy and unblameable and unreproveable in his sight: If ye continue in the faith grounded and settled, and be not moved away from the hope of the gospel, which ye have heard, and which was preached to every creature which is under heaven; whereof I Paul am made a minister;" (Colossians 1:19-23)

3)   **Make peace with others**. Follow Jesus when it comes to peace with people.

1. Jesus always saw people, even those that nobody else noticed (Zacchaeus; the woman at the well, the woman with the issue of blood...etc.)

i. Jesus noticed their need and potential.

Let's be aware of people in our homes, in our church, in our neighborhood and everywhere we go.

2. Jesus connected with people.
a. He found things that they had in common and focused on those.
b. He brought unusual people together to do miraculous things. He crossed the "lines of society." (There were no gender or racial lines to Jesus.)

Develop relationships with people.

3. Jesus engaged with people.
a. He invites people in. He invites them to peace. Jesus showed people that they mattered to Him.

Invite people to church, to your home, to activities with you. Invite them (most all) to a relationship with Jesus.

4. Jesus met the needs of people.
a. The greatest need we have is to be born again. He met that need and offered it to people.

It's okay to meet people's physical needs, but never leave off the gospel of Christ. Sometimes when people know that we care enough to meet a physical need, they are more likely to hear the truth of the Gospel.

4)   **Be willing to be the supposed villain.** Take risks and tell people about Jesus. Stand up for what the Bible says unapologetically. Be compassionate to ALL people. In this world, while there are some who are seeking peace and will embrace the message of

the gospel of peace, many will oppose it and fight against it. It is a risk to be a peacemaker. You won't always be seen as the "good guy." However, in the end, the one who brings peace to others is a reconciler, and the one who finds peace will be pleased. Besides that our God is pleased with the one who will tell others about Him —the way to peace.

It won't only be those who we try to reach with the gospel but those who are watching which may give us a hard time because our message is very different from the world. It's even different than what "religions" say today. We tell people of a relationship they can have with God. We tell them that there is a way to overcome addiction and social status, poverty, sin, hate...anything that is in the world. Those who have made a profit by keeping people down will not like the message of truth. Those who enjoy sin will not like the message of truth. Those who have the control now will not like the message of truth and peace. They didn't in Jesus' day either.

"Think not that I am come to send peace on earth: I came not to send peace, but a sword. For I am come to set a man at variance against his father, and the daughter against her mother, and the daughter in law against her mother in law. And a man's foes shall be they of his own household." (Matthew 10:34-36)

"Woe unto you, when all men shall speak well of you! for so did their fathers to the false prophets." (Luke 6:26)

"Rejoice, and be exceeding glad: for great is your reward in heaven: for so persecuted they the prophets which were before you." (Matthew 5:12)

"Follow peace with all men, and holiness, without which no man shall see the Lord:" (Hebrews 12:14

$$\sim 7 \sim$$

PART II: BIBLICAL EXAMPLE

John the Baptist—Peculiar yet Polarizing Peacemaking

Most of us have an idea of what we think a preacher looks like or have certain expectations regarding those who would be the peacemakers of the world. It was no different in the day of Jesus; however, John the Baptist proved to break the mold of what a preacher was.

The Bible describes him in Matthew 3: "In those days came John the Baptist, preaching in the wilderness of Judaea, And saying, Repent ye: for the kingdom of heaven is at hand. For this is he that was spoken of by the prophet Esaias, saying, The voice of one crying in the wilderness, Prepare ye the way of the Lord, make his paths straight. And the same John had his raiment of camel's hair, and a leathern girdle about his loins; and his meat was locusts and wild honey." (Matthew 3:1-4)

John held his church in the wilderness of Judaea, not in the temple as other preachers of his day. His message was simple: repent for the kingdom of God is at hand. His clothing was unusual —made of camel's hair and a leather belt. John's attire was part of his message: stand against worldly materialism.

His diet was also unusual compared to the rest of those of his occupation: locusts and wild honey. His diet was not indulgent but simple just like his clothing and his message.

Surely there were people who thought him strange, yet he was not without followers. In fact, many people came to hear his message and receive the peace that came from what John the Baptist offered—the kingdom of God.

"Then went out to him (John the Baptist) Jerusalem, and all Judaea, and all the region round about Jordan, And were baptized of him in Jordan, confessing their sins." (Matthew 3:5) People went to him from all around the area and got saved. They did what John preached—they repented of their sins (confessing their sins). They chose peace with God. Why? Because a strange preacher told them the truth—the kingdom of God was at hand.

Even the religious leaders went to John to be baptized, but his message, while still one of peace, was different to those leaders: "But when he saw many of the Pharisees and Sadducees come to his baptism, he said unto them, O generation of vipers, who hath warned you to flee from the wrath to come? Bring forth therefore fruits meet for repentance: And think not to say within yourselves, We have Abraham to our father: for I say unto you, that God is able of these stones to raise up children unto Abraham. And now also the axe is laid unto the root of the trees: therefore every tree which bringeth not forth good fruit is hewn down, and cast into the fire. I indeed baptize you with water unto repentance: but he that cometh after me is mightier than I, whose shoes I am not worthy to bear: he shall baptize you with the Holy Ghost, and with fire: Whose fan is in his hand, and he will throughly purge his floor, and gather his wheat into the garner; but he will burn up the chaff with unquenchable fire." (Matthew 3:7-12)

To some, John used simple words, "repent for the kingdom of heaven is at hand;" however, for the religious leaders, he found a need to be more direct. He did not address them in the usual honor that the Pharisees and Sadducees were accustomed to receiving. He did not change his message so that they would approve it. Instead, he called them out as children of the devil, "O generation of vipers."

You might say, are we still talking about peacemaking? Yes. John had the diligence to know that the Pharisees and Sadducees loved power. They loved their position, and they trusted in their family line and works for salvation. Therefore, at that point, they were unqualified for baptism. Again, it is faith in Jesus that saves. He told them "Bring forth therefore fruits meet for repentance," which means show that you agree with God—show that you have repented from your idolatry and self-righteousness. At that point, they were under the wrath of God, which John speaks of in verses 10-12. They could have no peace.

It might seem harsh, but peace does not come at the cost of getting along to get along. In fact, to do so would be endorsing sin and pushing people away from the peace of God. Peace comes with purity first. (James 3:17-18)

Purity starts in the heart, and it begins with God. It is by His standards. The Word of God tells us: "Keep yourselves in the love of God, looking for the mercy of our Lord Jesus Christ unto eternal life. And of some have compassion, making a difference: And others save with fear, pulling them out of the fire; hating even the garment spotted by the flesh." (Jude 21-23)

Though John was not in the preaching business to make friends but to build the kingdom of God, we find that he was a man of great influence with many followers; therefore, we can infer that John noticed people, that he connected with people, engaged with people, and met the needs of people.

In John, Chapter 1, the Jews sent priests and Levites from the capital city of Jerusalem to see if John was the Messiah. That's how large his influence and following was. "And this is the record of John, when the Jews sent priests and Levites from Jerusalem to ask him, Who art thou? And he confessed, and denied not; but confessed, I am not the Christ. And they asked him, What then? Art thou Elias? And he saith, I am not. Art thou that prophet? And he answered, No. Then said they unto him, Who art thou? that we may give an answer to them that sent us. What sayest thou of thyself?" (John 1:19-22)

In his response, though He didn't know Jesus (his cousin) was the Messiah, he pointed to the Messiah, the Promised One of God. "John answered them, saying, I baptize with water: but there standeth one among you, whom ye know not; He it is, who coming after me is preferred before me, whose shoe's latchet I am not worthy to unloose." (John 1:26-27)

Not only do we see a willingness to be odd for God and that John the Baptist was bold in the way that he spoke to the religious leaders, we also see that John was humble. John was not looking for recognition. Even his own followers, he pointed to Jesus once he knew who He was.

When Jesus stepped on the scene and John was given the sign from God that He is the Messiah (the Spirit descended upon Him like a dove), He began to point people to Jesus and away from himself. (John 1:29-34) "Again the next day after John stood, and two of his disciples; And looking upon Jesus as he walked, he saith, Behold the Lamb of God! And the two disciples heard him speak, and they followed Jesus." (John 1:35-37)

John's primary goal was just that—to point people to Jesus, to the kingdom of heaven—the way to peace, so he felt no jealousy or frustration that his disciples became Jesus' disciples. Those two disciples were in Jesus' close circle—Andrew, Simon Peter's brother and John the beloved, writer of John, 1st John, 2nd John, 3rd John, and Revelation.

John the Baptist's faithfulness in being a peacemaker begot more peacemakers. They went out and told other people about the way to peace, Jesus Christ—noticing people, connecting with people, engaging with people, and meeting the needs of people. He did it by being filled with the Spirit of God, not relying on himself or doing things for his honor or glory. It was by God and for God.

John took such great risks to see peace in the lives of others that he died for the cause, boldly proclaiming to King Herod that he was in sin and needed to repent. The king didn't repent, but he surely was convicted and did not lack respect for John the Baptist. In fact, it may have been that he believed John the Baptist to be the Messiah with the power to resurrect because after he murdered John for his brother's wife's sake, he wondered if Jesus was John the Baptist raised from the dead.

"At that time Herod the tetrarch heard of the fame of Jesus, And said unto his servants, This is John the Baptist; he is risen from the dead; and therefore mighty works do shew forth themselves in him. For Herod had laid hold on John, and bound him, and put him in prison for Herodias' sake, his brother Philip's wife. For John said unto him, It is not lawful for thee to have her. And when he would have put him to death, he feared the multitude, because they counted him as a prophet. But when Herod's birthday was kept, the daughter of Herodias danced before them, and pleased Herod. Whereupon he promised with an oath to give her whatsoever she would ask. And she, being before instructed of her mother, said, Give me here John Baptist's head in a charger. And the king was sorry: nevertheless for the oath's sake, and them which sat with him at meat, he commanded it to be given her. And he sent, and beheaded John in the prison. And his head was brought in a charger, and given to the damsel: and she brought it to her mother." (Matthew 14:1-11)

You might say that is a sad ending for John the Baptist, the peacemaker, but it was no different than Jesus, the prophets who went before them, and the many peacemakers who came after, including all of the disciples except John the beloved. There is a cost to being a peacemaker. However, there is a great reward to being a peacemaker. It was no doubt that John the Baptist was a child of God. "Blessed are the peacemakers: for they shall be called the children of God." (Matthew 5:9) Jesus even said of John the Baptist: "Verily I say unto you, Among them that are born of women there hath not risen a greater than John the Baptist: notwithstanding he that is least in the kingdom of heaven is greater than he." (Matthew 11:11)

Consider that statement. Jesus saw John the Baptist as a great man because of his heart toward God and the people that went to God and received peace with God because of his life. However, He says

"notwithstanding he that is least in the kingdom of heaven is greater than he." (Matthew 11:11b) I believe that he is talking about all those that came after Jesus died for our sins, was buried and resurrected and ascended back to heaven. There is a greater power now. The message now is that the kingdom of God is here, and Jesus will return. Repent before it is too late.

John had the Spirit of God. He had a special calling from God before the ministry of the Holy Spirit that we have today. We can see that God was with John. That was not true of everyone in that day. The Holy Spirit did not work like He does now. Now, all we who believe have the Holy Spirit of God and are able to minister reconciliation to all people.

We have the power of God. We have the Word of God in its complete form. We have roads and technology that the people of John's day, and for centuries beyond, could never dream of. Yet, do we see reconciliation like those times? Do we see people flocking to the people of God because of a power within that they do not have and they desire? No. Why not? Because all of those luxuries and technologies that we have, have become idols to us instead of means to share the good news of God.

May we go without like John the Baptist did so that people can see that there is true peace with God. May we decrease that Christ might increase.

$$\sim 7 \sim$$

PART II: BIBLICAL EXAMPLE

Peter—from hiding to reconciling

Peter was a disciple of Jesus Christ. He was actually fruit of John the Baptist's peacemaking ministry. Andrew, Peter's brother, was a disciple of John, and when John pointed him to the Messiah, Andrew immediately found his brother to take him to Jesus. "One of the two which heard John speak, and followed him, was Andrew, Simon Peter's brother. He first findeth his own brother Simon, and saith unto him, We have found the Messias, which is, being interpreted, the Christ. And he brought him to Jesus." (John 1:40-42)

Peter was bold and full of faith, but he found himself quiet and ashamed on the day that Jesus was taken captive by the Jewish leaders. When asked if he was a follower of Jesus, he denied Jesus three times (just as Jesus said he would). "And Simon Peter followed Jesus, and so did another disciple: that disciple was known unto the high priest, and went in with Jesus into the palace of the high priest. But Peter stood at the door without. Then went out that other disciple, which was known unto the high priest, and spake unto her that kept the door, and brought in Peter. Then saith the damsel that kept the door unto Peter, Art not thou also one of this man's disciples? He saith, I am not. And the servants and officers stood there, who had made a fire of coals; for it was cold: and they warmed themselves: and Peter stood with them, and warmed himself." (John 18:15-18)

"And Simon Peter stood and warmed himself. They said therefore unto him, Art not thou also one of his disciples? He denied it, and said, I am not. One of the servants of the high priest, being his kinsman whose ear Peter cut off, saith, Did not I see thee in the garden with him? Peter then denied again: and immediately the cock crew." (John 18:25-27)

To know Peter, this was a surprise. It was, no doubt, a surprise even to Peter himself who claimed that he would die with Jesus when Jesus told him this prophesy. Fear had gotten the best of Peter. He was unsure of all the things that he thought he believed. Peace was replaced with the sin of fear, doubt, unbelief and shame.

We are no better than this disciple who spent intimate time with the Savior. There are situations that rock us to our core and make us question our faith. Our peace can be pushed in the back of our hearts as fear takes the front seat. While it might be a surprise to us, it is no surprise to God, just like Peter's denial was no surprise to Jesus.

Peter, even after seeing Jesus more than once after He rose from the dead, found himself backslidden. He was still unsure about how to move on with Jesus away. He did not yet understand what Jesus had told him regarding the Holy Spirit and how He would leave them but not without another Comforter. So, Peter went fishing.

"After these things Jesus shewed himself again to the disciples at the sea of Tiberias; and on this wise shewed he himself. There were together Simon Peter, and Thomas called Didymus, and Nathanael of Cana in Galilee, and the sons of Zebedee, and two other of his disciples. Simon Peter saith unto them, I go a fishing. They say unto him, We also go with thee. They went forth, and entered into a ship immediately; and that night they caught nothing." (John 21:1-3)

Part of our natural thinking has us turn to the old things when we get fearful or aren't sure about things. Let's recall that it will lead to nothing, just like Peter and the other disciples that night.

As they were returning to shore, Jesus called out to them. Peter immediately gird himself (put on clothing fit to be in the presence of the Savior) and jumped into the water to swim to meet Jesus. It was no doubt that Peter loved Jesus. Yet, he had a lot of himself that needed to take a backseat and he needed to trust God and live by faith.

Jesus told Peter back before he denied Him: "And the Lord said, Simon, Simon, behold, Satan hath desired to have you, that he may sift you as wheat: But I have prayed for thee, that thy faith fail not: and when thou art converted, strengthen thy brethren. And he said unto him, Lord, I am ready to go with thee, both into prison, and to death. And he said, I tell thee, Peter, the cock shall not crow this day, before that thou shalt thrice deny that thou knowest me." (Luke 22:31-34)

Jesus, no doubt, has similar words for us (at least regarding the first part of this passage). The enemy of our souls certainly desires to sift us as wheat. Jesus certainly prays for us. When we are converted, Jesus wants us to strengthen fellow believers.

Converted means to turn back; to be changed. Jesus knew Peter's heart, and He knows ours. There are times where we need to be converted to the Lord...again. Until then, we will not be able to be peacemakers. At that time, Peter was not a peacemaker. He, in fact, took people fishing with him, and that is when Jesus took Peter aside and told him basically, 'if you love me, strengthen the brethren' (feed my sheep).

By the day of Pentecost, there could be no doubt that Peter was fully converted. He had turned back to Jesus and was once again that bold, unashamed disciple full of faith like that faith Jesus told us that He would build His church on. In one day, Peter preached and at least 3,000 people got saved. 3,000 people found reconciliation with God. 3,000 people finally had peace with God and had the ability to have peace with others. Amen! What a miracle!

"But Peter, standing up with the eleven, lifted up his voice, and said unto them, Ye men of Judaea, and all ye that dwell at

Jerusalem, be this known unto you, and hearken to my words:... Men and brethren, let me freely speak unto you of the patriarch David, that he is both dead and buried, and his sepulchre is with us unto this day. Therefore being a prophet, and knowing that God had sworn with an oath to him, that of the fruit of his loins, according to the flesh, he would raise up Christ to sit on his throne; He seeing this before spake of the resurrection of Christ, that his soul was not left in hell, neither his flesh did see corruption. This Jesus hath God raised up, whereof we all are witnesses. Therefore being by the right hand of God exalted, and having received of the Father the promise of the Holy Ghost, he hath shed forth this, which ye now see and hear. For David is not ascended into the heavens: but he saith himself, The LORD said unto my Lord, Sit thou on my right hand, Until I make thy foes thy footstool. Therefore let all the house of Israel know assuredly, that God hath made that same Jesus, whom ye have crucified, both Lord and Christ. Now when they heard this, they were pricked in their heart, and said unto Peter and to the rest of the apostles, Men and brethren, what shall we do? Then Peter said unto them, Repent, and be baptized every one of you in the name of Jesus Christ for the remission of sins, and ye shall receive the gift of the Holy Ghost. For the promise is unto you, and to your children, and to all that are afar off, even as many as the Lord our God shall call. And with many other words did he testify and exhort, saying, Save yourselves from this untoward generation. Then they that gladly received his word were baptized: and the same day there were added unto them about three thousand souls." (Acts 2:14; 29-41—Read Acts 2 for the entire context)

Peter wasn't soft. He didn't only speak of the love of God. Peter said some things that were hard to hear. The people were "pricked in their hearts." Yet, they came to the saving knowledge of Jesus that day. May we choose to be real with people about God. Yes, He is love, but in His love, He must judge sin. In His love, He has made a way to escape that judgement, being His only begotten Son dying for our sin. In His love, He gives a new nature to all of we who will believe on His Son, and we will then have the power over sin where it doesn't have dominion in our lives.

It was not Peter's power that brought 3,000 people to know Jesus that day. It was not Peter at all, really. Peter was used by God to be a vessel that spoke into the hearts of those people, and it was God that convicted and called. The God of peace brought peace to many souls that day, and those souls became peacemakers, or at least had the ability to become peacemakers.

I love that God found it necessary to put Peter's hiccups in the Word of God for us. If all we saw was the time that he stepped out on water but not the moment that he took his eyes off Jesus and began to sink, we might think there is no hope for us. If all we knew about Peter was that in one day preaching, 3,000 people got saved, we might think God only calls great and mighty people.

The truth is God calls people who need Him. We all need Him. We all can find ourselves backslidden at times, and when we get converted—when we turn ourselves back to the Lord, we can go back to being peacemakers for the Lord so that we can be known as children of God. That was Peter's testimony to those around him: "Now when they saw the boldness of Peter and John, and perceived that they were unlearned and ignorant men, they marvelled; and they took knowledge of them, that they had been with Jesus." (Acts 4:13)

~ 7 ~

PART III: PERSONAL EXAMPLE

From Peace destroyer to Peacekeeper to Peacemaker

You've probably heard the saying hurt people hurt people. With a lack of peace within comes a lack of peace without. By the time I was seven years old, that lack of peace within started to come out. I can see now that sin was the enemy even back then, but in my young mind, I developed a mistrust of adults because people who were entrusted to care for me severally betrayed my trust. I also developed a protective shell against my peers because I always felt like an outsider.

Confused and angry, I would almost dare people to start a fight with me. From my turmoil within, to the fighting at home, to the fighting outside of the home, I had no clue that peace was a reality in anybody's life.

My seven-year-old self wanted peace; I'm sure. My family was hurting. It made me hurt. I remember very vividly a D.A.R.E (Drug Abuse Resistance Education) class that we had to take. It may have been third grade (so eight years old). I went away from that class concerned about family members which I knew were taking drugs. I was afraid that they were going to die. I wrote them all tear-stained letters begging them to quit.

Of course, that seems easy to a little girl, but my heart broke that they didn't quit the drugs. In fact, I watched as the adults in my life continued to indulge in harmful, dangerous behaviors. It wasn't long before I embraced those behaviors as fun ways to interact with others and eventually took up some of those habits for myself.

By the time I was fourteen, nobody had to coerce me into taking my first hit of marijuana. I did it all by myself. I adopted the way that the adults around me found peace. (Let that be a lesson to us all. Our sinful habits do hurt those who follow us. Of course, on the other side of that coin, our good habits do help those who follow us!) In fact, I was the one who got others to try it with me. I pushed what I thought was bringing peace to me upon others who looked up to me—People whom I had relationships with because I saw them, connected with them, engaged with them and met their needs. I'm ashamed of that now. For eighteen years marijuana was a god to me. It was a stronghold that I went to when I needed peace, when I needed happiness, when I needed comfort, when I needed fun...etc.

By the time I was a young adult, I had my heart broken several times and broke a couple hearts myself. I had gone to college where I did things that only left me feeling shame and guilt. Those foolish decisions put me in a position where my guard was down and one of my deepest scars were formed. It was in those days that I needed more than marijuana, and alcohol became more of a stronghold for me.

Alcohol was not silent in the fact that it was an enemy of mine, and though I didn't quit drinking altogether, I slowed down my drinking fearful of being unable to stop. I found what I thought was a balance. However, chaos, disturbance, and war followed every-where I went. I had never known peace, and so when I got to the point where I was drinking more, having more violent spurts, and thinking of harming myself, I knew I had to try something else.

I was thirty-two years old, pregnant again, and as I mentioned before, I had no hope for life anymore. Without those substances that I had relied on (because I was pregnant), I could feel every feeling and comprehend every thought. I had to deal with what was going on with me. I had to confront my thoughts, feelings, and desires and decided I wanted a different future than where I was headed. That made me turn to God.

On that morning/afternoon, life changed. What peace fills your soul when you realize that the God of heaven heard you! As I prayed to God and my phone rang with an invite to church, I was sure God answered my prayer.

Hearing God's heart through the preaching made me desire to give Him everything. The day that I surrendered, my pastor at the time was preaching from the parable of the Sower and the Seed. (Matthew 13:3-9; 18-23)

I'll never forget that because it was so real to me. I had been in church before. I liked church. I liked hearing the Word of God. I was even pulled toward it, but I often let the cares of the world, or my love of the world, choke every desire of God out of me; and the fruit that was my life at that time was not valuable, so I decided that I wanted to be one who allowed the Word to land on the good ground of my heart that I might have good fruit.

Tears flooded my face as I thought about all those times that God called out to me and pulled at my heart but I ignored Him. I ached as I reminisced in my mind of those times that He even spoke to me to go another way while I walked directly into danger. I prayed and surrendered to God that day at church and while I don't have it all together, I know what the peace of God is.

It was like God reached down and lifted every burden off my shoulder. I don't want to give an idea that it's all emotion and feelings when we get right with the Lord because not everyone has the same experience, but this is my experience. I got up from that alter twenty pounds lighter. I finally felt safe in my spirit, mind, and body—I had peace.

That day I went from pushing the only way to peace that I had known before, which was all destructive things, to pushing Jesus and the peace that He brings which is real. My family and friends were still coming over to the house every day, but I was different. The usual interests were no longer acceptable in my home. I just wanted to celebrate life—with them.

My behavior more than my words, surely, was what everyone noticed, so I told them about Jesus—the source of my change. I spoke and showed that I had a new source of peace that was truly working. I offered them Jesus. Nearly every one of my family members who were coming around came to church with me at least a couple of times. Some even proclaimed to have accepted Jesus as Savior.

Once the honeymoon stage was over, so to speak, people started to try to pull me back into the old way of life. They weren't very fond of the new me. Because my family is dear to me and I felt like I was losing them, I spent some time being a peacekeeper. I allowed the things that I wasn't for anymore just to have them around, and though I wasn't tempted to go back to the old life much, it did begin to vex my soul. I would feel conflicted, and it was blocking growth in my life. It was the RU verses that finally got me to step back more. "Blessed is the man that walketh not in the counsel of the ungodly, nor standeth in the way of sinners, nor sitteth in the seat of the scornful. But his delight is in the law of the LORD; and in his law doth he meditate day and night." (Psalm 1:1-2)

I began to change my focus to my studies, church attendance, and ministry. I still tried to make some time to be a witness to family. I invited them to church often. However, it wasn't long before those people stopped coming around the house and ignored my invites to church or bible study together.

I was starting to learn that peacemaking isn't always bringing what we think of as peace at the start. In fact, many of my old relationships with friends and family broke. We fell apart. We weren't headed in the same direction, and it became very hard to be together.

I started this year (2022) with a heart's desire to reach people. I wanted to impact lives for Jesus. I wanted to bring peace to people's lives, so I prayed and asked God to restore relationships. I had written letters to a few family members in hopes to let them know that I was sorry for my part in our broken relationship. Before long, God opened doors that I thought were shut. My mom, siblings and nieces and nephews (on my mom's side) have been having monthly game nights. I have met with friends from church once a week in Bible study and fellowship. I have even developed a strong relationship with an old friend whom I've known for 30 years.

I feel like this chapter isn't quite ready to be published. I am standing on faith and not compromising. I talk about Jesus and give the peace prescription often, but many of my family still haven't accepted the peace that comes from knowing Jesus. I have not given up, and I will not give up. I believe that my seeing people, connecting with people, engaging with people, and meeting the needs of people is going to have fruit of peace in their lives when they're ready.

I am excited that my 30-year friendship is starting to develop into a very close friendship and discipleship where she is seeking God and starting to embrace God's ways. I could've never had this position if I would've focused on our differences or on the things and ways of the world. I never stopped reaching out to her, and we continued our friendship even after I started seeing things differently than she did politically. While that was breaking relationships around the nation, we didn't break; we may have had some disagreements but always remained friends.

About six months ago this friend reached out to me, and we began talking again. She said she was tired and needed help. I had been trying to disciple a few people up to that point and had actually given up looking for someone to invest in spiritually. I was just praying. (Another lesson learned to wait on God.) God united us once again. I invited her to lunch and brought up discipleship.

She agreed to the discipleship which calls for Bible study throughout the week, and we meet once a week to discuss the Bible study and life and come up with some goals moving forward. Two weeks into the discipleship, she realized that she was not a child of God. She cried out to the Lord to save her while in the privacy of her own house one night while reviewing the Scriptures. Amen!

We are still on this journey of discipleship, and I am blessed to be able to go through it with her. I am not special. She's not special; however, knowing the Lord of peace changes things. I have no doubt that God is going to do something special in her life as she gets to know the God of peace and receives that peace unto herself. She will be an amazing peacemaker, known as a child of God. Amen!

How is this a possibility? I got to know the God of peace who taught me peace. I began to seek Truth until I could speak Truth and then I started to share the truth that I learned with others.

The same will be true for my family. Even when I think of my oldest son who has turned away from God, I trust that having a relationship with God and remaining close to Him, seeing my son where he is and loving him where he is, while connecting in the things that we have in common and engaging him, willing to meet needs when I can, will eventually bring him to a place where he will choose the peace of God.

Sometimes peace comes through discomfort or strife. I had let things get out of hand over the last few years in my home. Everyone has gotten comfortable and does what he/she feels. My relationship with them was collapsing and their relationships with each other were falling apart as well. The home had become chaotic, and sin had crept in, therefore peace has become rare in our home. Something had to change, and it was going to have to be me that initiated it.

God has been speaking to me throughout this whole process, but I found it overwhelming. Finally, He gave me the truth (or perhaps it is that I accepted the truth) that He has called me to this therefore I can do it IN HIM. (1 Thessalonians 5:14; Philippians 1:6, Exodus 4:10-11)

I began to pray that the Lord would prepare my heart and the kids' hearts that I would approach the change in a loving way. After two weeks of prayer, I, against all feelings, called a family meeting where I discussed that it was time for them to do the things expected of them. I reviewed what those things were, and I made it clear that there would be consequences when those expectations were not met.

I wish that I can say that I have been perfect on this thing. I haven't, but I have been aware and consistent in giving consequences when expectations are not met. This, of course, has challenges, but surprisingly I am not met with hostility as I was assuming it would be.

In fact, most of the conflict and struggle is within myself. I have to get over my comfort and take the time to inspect what I expect in order to be consistent. I have to be willing to have hard conversations at times and be willing to deal with bad attitudes. I have to give out punishments when needed. I have to push past my fear of pushing my children away.

I know, however, that I can trust the Lord more than my own understanding or even experience in life. His Word tells me not to leave my children alone (Proverbs 29:15), to discipline them (Proverbs 23:13-14; Proverbs 29:17), and to raise them up to love Him (Deuteronomy 6:5-7) and there will be rewards (Proverbs 22:6;).

I desire to be bolder and tell much more people about Jesus. He is the way to peace. He is the answer to every problem that is taking over our lives in America today. The atmosphere is dark and tight in our nation, but the Light of the world is ready to shine into every heart. We just have to have the Light in us, yield to Him, and let Him shine through us.

It won't be easy. Everyone will not accept the message. In fact, many will not. It didn't stop Jesus from willingly going to the cross to bring peace to those who will accept. It didn't stop all of the prophets before Jesus. It didn't stop those who came after Him. It shouldn't stop us.

I feel like I have a long way to go before I will be called a peacemaker, but I am willing to work toward that. Right now I am praying and starting to restore old relationships and get out more to develop new relationships. Peacemaking is a process, and it is more efficient with relationships.

We are at a time where there is no greater need in the world than peace aka Jesus, the God of peace. So many are taken to a false peace or seeking a false peace—unity of religion, no racism at all, no poverty, acceptance of all people in all things—these are not at all a reality. They will never be. So, instead of people seeking after true peace, they are seeking something that will never come, and disappointment and more chaos are the only things that will.

Judgment is coming soon. We need to be ready. We need to warn people that they may be safe at that time. There was to be a judgment during the days that Jeremiah was preaching. Apparently, the world was a lot like it is now—everybody looking in other directions for peace and falsely believing that those things bring peace. Even many who claim to preach the Word of God seem to be looking at the government or social programs for peace. "For from the least of them even unto the greatest of them every one is given to covetousness; and from the prophet even unto the priest every one dealeth falsely. They have healed also the hurt of the daughter of my people slightly, saying, Peace, peace; when there is no peace. Were they ashamed when they had committed abomination? nay, they were not at all ashamed, neither could they blush: therefore they shall fall among them that fall: at the time that I visit them they shall be cast down, saith the LORD. Thus saith the LORD, Stand ye in the ways, and see, and ask for the old paths, where is the good way, and walk therein, and ye shall find rest for your souls. But they said, We will not walk therein." (Jeremiah 6:13-16)

There must first be purity before peace (James 3:17). Unfortunately, the search for peace in the world has delivered up more impurity bringing sin which brings death. (James 1:15) We are exalting people who are wise in their own eyes instead of the One who is wisdom—Jesus Christ. What does the Bible say about that?

"The wicked walk on every side, when the vilest men are exalted." (Psalm 12:8)

In order to be peacemakers, we must be willing to be different, even be hated by the world for a while, just like our Savior. We must ask ourselves are we being peacemakers. Are we peace destroyers? Are we peacekeepers? Or Are we peacemakers, where we will be known as the children of God (Matthew 5:9)?

"As I have said, the first thing is to be honest with yourself. You can never have an impact on society if you have not changed yourself... Great peacemakers are all people of integrity, of honesty, but humility." – Nelson Mandela

"Peace is a daily, a weekly, a monthly process, gradually changing opinions, slowly eroding old barriers, quietly building new structures." – John F. Kennedy

"Darkness cannot drive out darkness; only light can do that. Hate cannot drive out hate; only love can do that." – Martin Luther King, Jr.

"Those who love peace must learn to organize as effectively as those who love war." – Martin Luther King, Jr.

"Be a peacemaker but never at the expense of your character or God's standards." – Jim George

PART IV: GO DEEPER

1. Compare the world's definition of peace with the Biblical definition of peace. First, look up peace in an ordinary dictionary. Then, look up a Biblical definition of peace or use the one found in this chapter of the book.

   a. Peace (world's definition)—

   ----

   b. Peace (Biblical definition)—

   ----

   c. What are the similarities? Differences?

   ----

   d. Which peace comes to mind when you think of peace?

   ----

2. Do the same for peacemaker as you've done above (in number 1.).

   a. Peacemaker (world's definition)—

---

b. Peacemaker (Biblical definition)—

---

c. What are the similarities? Differences?

---

3. How does peacemaker compare to peacekeeper?

---

4. Have you been more of a peacekeeper or peacemaker? Why do you think that is?

---

5. What must we have in order to be a peacemaker?

---

6. How do we receive that (what it takes to be a peacemaker)? Write the Bible verse(s) that helps you know that and that you can use to tell others (how they can get to a place where they can be a peacemaker)?

----

7. Consider the following passage and answer the questions that follow.

a. "Now we exhort you, brethren, warn them that are unruly, comfort the feebleminded, support the weak, be patient toward all men. 1Th 5:14

b. See that none render evil for evil unto any man; but ever follow that which is good, both among yourselves, and to all men. 1Th 5:15

c. Rejoice evermore. 1Th 5:16

d. Pray without ceasing. 1Th 5:17

e. In every thing give thanks: for this is the will of God in Christ Jesus concerning you. 1Th 5:18

f. Quench not the Spirit. 1Th 5:19

g. Despise not prophesyings. 1Th 5:20

h. Prove all things; hold fast that which is good. 1Th 5:21

i. Abstain from all appearance of evil. 1Th 5:22

j. And the very God of peace sanctify you wholly; and I pray God your whole spirit and soul and body be preserved blameless unto the coming of our Lord Jesus Christ. 1Th 5:23

k. Faithful is he that calleth you, who also will do it." 1Th 5:24

8. In verses 14-15, we see how we Christians should treat all people. What are the five commands that we see in those two verses?

1)____

____

2)____

____

3)____

____

4)____

____

5)____

____

9. Look at each command and (1) write what it means (use your Bible dictionary) and (2) a way that you personally can do that command and (3) how it makes you a peacemaker. (You may need to review how Jesus showed us how to be a peacemaker)

1)

(1)   ____

(2)   ____

(3)   ____

2)   (1)_______________________________________

(2)   ____

(3)   ____

3)   (1)_______________________________________

(2)   ____

(3)   ____

4)   (1)_______________________________________

(2)   ____

(3)   ____

5)   (1)_______________________________________

____

(2) _______________________________________

____

(3) _______________________________________

____

10. In verses 16-22, what commands are mentioned?

1) _______________________________________

2) _______________________________________

3) _______________________________________

4) _______________________________________

5) _______________________________________

6) _______________________________________

7) _______________________________________

11. How do you think putting those commands to use in our lives will make us more effective peacemakers?

____

____

____

____

12. According to verses 23 and 24, what blessings can we count on IF we do those things mentioned in the verses before?

____

____

____

13. What are the four things Jesus demonstrated of how we can be a peacemaker among others?

1) _______________________________________

2) _______________________________________

3) _______________________________________

4) _______________________________________

14. Is it true that being a peacemaker means that we are free from any trouble or conflict with others? Why or why not?

____

____

____

15. Consider the passage below and answer the following questions.

"Now no chastening for the present seemeth to be joyous, but grievous: nevertheless afterward it yieldeth the peaceable fruit of righteousness unto them which are exercised thereby. Wherefore lift up the hands which hang down, and the feeble knees; And make straight paths for your feet, lest that which is lame be turned out of the way; but let it rather be healed. Follow peace with all men, and holiness, without which no man shall see the Lord:" (Hebrews 12:11-14)

1. What do you think chastening of the Lord or of a person has to do with peace in your own life? (look up chastening if you are not sure what it means)

____

____

____

2. How is chastening first described?

____

____

____

3. Nevertheless, the Bible tells us, what will be the result of chastening when taken properly?

____

____

____

4. What is the only way a person can see the Lord?

____

____

____

5. Considering the above verses, do you think that being a peacemaker is always about saying things that others will consider pleasing? Why or why not?

____

____

----

16. As you start or continue your journey of peacemaking, remember these verses: "Open rebuke is better than secret love. Faithful are the wounds of a friend; but the kisses of an enemy are deceitful." (Proverbs 27:5-6) It is our nature to think that bringing peace must be a compromise or should never involve anything uncomfortable or conflicting. Study these verses out and write what it means below.

~ 8 ~

BLESSED ARE THE PERSECUTED
FOR RIGHTEOUSNESS' SAKE

Part I—INSIGHT: Gaining Knowledge

"Blessed are they which are persecuted for righteousness' sake: for theirs is the kingdom of heaven." (Matthew 5:10)

When we started this journey at looking at true happiness in our lives, I mentioned that oftentimes what Jesus says to us goes against our natural way of thinking. I want to reiterate that here. This attitude of being happy when we are persecuted for righteousness' sake seems crazy. Let's look at what this means and how we can see it in our lives.

First, let's remember that blessed or happy is what we are. It is not based on our feelings or circumstances. It is an internal blessing from our Savior. If it wouldn't have made it confusing, I would use the word joy throughout this book because God's happiness, in reality, is joy. It is a fruit of the Spirit of God working in our lives as we yield to Him.

No matter what, this happiness/joy is available. We often forfeit the access to it because we are too concerned with feelings or circumstances in this temporary world. No doubt if we find ourselves being persecuted for doing something for the kingdom of God, we can have emotions that don't scream "I'm happy!".

Persecuted is often misused. Some people think that persecution is only big stuff like being martyred or jailed for sharing the gospel. While that is certainly persecution, we can be persecuted in small ways that trip us up and distract us from God's calling.

Biblically the word persecuted means harassed by troubles or punishments unjustly inflicted, particularly for religious opinions. Persecution targets an individual not because they are doing evil, not because they have hurt others but simply for their faith. In fact, our key text tells us, "Blessed are they which are persecuted for righteousness' sake."

If you have had such kingdom-minded attitudes through your life that you find yourself persecuted, truly you are in a special group of people. This is not for all people who claim Christianity, and it is not something that we see from the beginning of our walks because persecuted people are those who have demonstrated they are on God's side. They show that they are poor in spirit, they mourn over their sin, they are meek and have their desire after righteousness. They have proved that they are merciful, pure in heart and peacemakers; therefore, they are persecuted.

Persecution is a mark of someone who has really allowed God to invade their lives and use them for His kingdom. "Yea, and all that will live godly in Christ Jesus shall suffer persecution." (2 Timothy 3:12).

From the beginning we see persecution to those who are righteous. The first-born man killed the second-born man simply for righteousness' sake.

Why? Not everyone handles conviction properly. God convicts us to bring us to Him; however, some go the other way and can only hear the condemnation of the enemy which makes them hate God and all that is good. There are some that knowingly love darkness; therefore, they seek to squash all light in the world.

Either way it comes down to it not being a personal thing for any of us. It wasn't personal for Able that Cain killed him.

It was a spiritual battle. It was deeper than the two men. When we are persecuted, it's not about us personally; it's about the message and the Person of the message—Jesus Christ. "For we wrestle not against flesh and blood, but against principalities, against powers, against the rulers of the darkness of this world, against spiritual wickedness in high places." (Ephesians 6:12)

So, why would persecution make us happy?

It's not the persecution that makes us happy. It's the place that we are in to find ourselves persecuted that should help us recognize that we are blessed. If the enemy has taken notice, how much more has our God? "Many are the afflictions of the righteous: but the LORD delivereth him out of them all." (Psalm 34:19)

There is always a purpose in all that God does, and that is to bring people to Him. Persecution is not enjoyable, but if we get to the place where we are persecuted, we have seen God work mightily. We know of His goodness, power, and deliverance, and we must stay focused on Him that He will work in and through us and receive glory in those who are watching.

Paul went from being a persecutor to being persecuted and he wrote, "But we have this treasure in earthen vessels, that the excellency of the power may be of God, and not of us. We are troubled on every side, yet not distressed; we are perplexed, but not in despair; Persecuted, but not forsaken; cast down, but not destroyed; Always bearing about in the body the dying of the Lord Jesus, that the life also of Jesus might be made manifest in our body." (2 Corinthians 4:7-10)

Paul was basically saying, 'yeah, there's a lot going on. There is trouble all around us, yet we know that God got us; therefore, we keep preaching and showing the goodness of God so that people will see Jesus through us.'

So, when it comes to persecution there is a realization that it is inevitable, there is a reason for it (God has a purpose), and there is a response that all Christians should have. If you have noticed, there is a progression of attitude in the be-attitudes, and through it all we need the Lord to guide us in them.

First, being poor in spirit is that initial and everyday recognition that we need God—that there are bigger things that we need in life (love, joy (God-given happiness), peace, acceptance, forgiveness, comfort...) that only truly come from knowing God. That attitude gets us to seek God more and embrace His teachings and judgments as the way, the truth, and the life. (John 14:6)

Secondly, we begin to mourn over our sin, recognizing that we have sinned against a holy and righteous God who loves us and desires what's best for us. This also makes us draw closer to God as we receive His comfort.

Then we find ourselves being meek or gentle with others, realizing that others need this mercy and love as well, so we humbly respond to others and try to show them the One who gives an abundant life (John 10:10).

We notice that our desires begin to change, and we no longer value those things that we used to; instead, we hunger and thirst after righteousness and find ourselves satisfied. Once again, this makes us draw closer to God, as He transforms us and changes our thoughts, feelings, and desires to see His kingdom above our own kingdom that we were trying to build before.

We then find ourselves showing mercy as we never had before. We likely see lives changing because of the change that He has done in us, and those that we see whom are hurting, we desire to see them get to know the One who can make a difference in their lives.

See, what is happening is that we, at that point, are far less like the world, and people notice. Some become convicted of their own sin and either get right with the Lord or count you as one who thinks you are better than them or against them. It is at this attitude point that no one can say that you are acting any longer—we set ourselves apart from those who are trying in their own power because all of the previous attitudes can be faked for a while, but mercy is not something our natural man can make up. It is genuine and sincere. It comes from a heart that agrees with God.

The world doesn't mind someone who is imitating Christ. They love those people. However, when we become more like Christ and they can see Christ in us, they will hate us. "These things I command you, that ye love one another. If the world hate you, ye know that it hated me before it hated you. If ye were of the world, the world would love his own: but because ye are not of the world, but I have chosen you out of the world, therefore the world hateth you. Remember the word that I said unto you, The servant is not greater than his lord. If they have persecuted me, they will also persecute you; if they have kept my saying, they will keep yours also. But all these things will they do unto you for my name's sake, because they know not him that sent me." (John 15:17-21).

What a paradox is the kingdom of God! At least to our natural minds. God's ways are higher than ours (Isaiah 55:9) and He uses the paradox to bring people to Him (1 Corinthians 1:27-31), which is always the goal (John 3:16-17; 2 Peter 3:9).

Jesus told us that people are going to hate us because of Him. He has given us an example that we cannot be above. He also gave us the way to go through the persecution, even if it is to death, knowing that we have a great reward in heaven. Yet, many might say, "don't sign me up for that." I mean that is what our natural mind would think, but do you know throughout history, since the beginning of time, when God's people were persecuted, the church grew—more people came to know the Savior in such time instead of less. I cannot explain it, but, again, God's ways are higher.

Jesus also told us, "These things I have spoken unto you, that in me ye might have peace. In the world ye shall have tribulation: but be of good cheer; I have overcome the world." (John 16:33) In Him, we will have peace, even though there is tribulation and persecution. How? He has already overcome the world and every other enemy we have, and He is within us. Amen! "Ye are of God, little children, and have overcome them: because greater is he that is in you, than he that is in the world." (1 John 4:4)

Persecution is inevitable to the one who is close to Jesus.

Mercy begins to separate the imitators from those who are walking with God, and then as we continuously draw closer to the Lord, we become pure in heart. Impurities start to burn away, oftentimes under the heat of persecution as we see God in and through those fiery trials. "Beloved, think it not strange concerning the fiery trial which is to try you, as though some strange thing happened unto you: But rejoice, inasmuch as ye are partakers of Christ's sufferings; that, when his glory shall be revealed, ye may be glad also with exceeding joy. If ye be reproached for the name of Christ, happy are ye; for the spirit of glory and of God resteth upon you: on their part he is evil spoken of, but on your part he is glorified." (1 Peter 4:12-14)

From the last two chapters we know that purity in heart leads to peacemaking, where a lot of times we have to go through some conflict in order to see righteousness in the hearts of those around us. That conflict is often persecution. Why? Because we are known as the children of God.

~ 8 ~

PART I (CONTINUED)

"Blessed are they which are persecuted for righteousness' sake: for theirs is the kingdom of heaven." (Matthew 5:10)

"Blessed are they which are persecuted for righteousness' sake: for theirs is the kingdom of heaven. Blessed are ye, when men shall revile you, and persecute you, and shall say all manner of evil against you falsely, for my sake. Rejoice, and be exceeding glad: for great is your reward in heaven: for so persecuted they the prophets which were before you." (Matthew 5:10-12)

Persecution probably takes the cake of something that isn't plausible would bring you true happiness. It is ironic and doesn't make sense in our minds.

First thing to note, Christian, is this is war. There is spiritual warfare every day. Our enemy battles to keep people blind and falsely happy on their way to hell. "But if our gospel be hid, it is hid to them that are lost: In whom the god of this world hath blinded the minds of them which believe not, lest the light of the glorious gospel of Christ, who is the image of God, should shine unto them." (2 Corinthians 4:3-4) This is Satan's territory that we are in right now, and he doesn't play fair.

Praise God, though, that He didn't send us out here alone. We have a greater power in us, and we win in the end. We can carry that victory through every battle that we face today, too.

160

Yes, we might see some defeats along the way, likely because we get away from the Commander in Chief (Jesus), but there will be a lot more victories the closer we remain to Jesus.

It's important that we know this so that it can start to make a little sense to us as to why it is more difficult for the Christian on earth than the one who is without Christ—why it is that God's people are the ones who are persecuted and not the enemies' children. Our glory and blessings are nothing to compare to our present sufferings (2 Corinthians 4:17); however, the blessings and glory that the lost person has on earth are nothing compared to the eternal torments they will have to endure (see Lazarus and the rich man in Luke 16:19-31).

We looked at the inevitability of persecution for the one who allows God to grow him/her through the transforming power of the Word of God and teaching and leading of the Holy Spirit. What are those persecutions, the purpose in them, and the perpetual blessings that come from being in this place of persecuted for righteousness' sake? The next verses give more insight.

"Blessed are ye, when men shall revile you, and persecute you, and shall say all manner of evil against you falsely, for my sake" (Matthew 5:11) Reviling is mentioned here. Reviling means taunt with words—a person speaks of you with disdain and reproach, speaks little of you. Surely, we see that the world reviles Christians and Christianity every day. According to the world, Christians are judgmental, self-centered, racist, bigoted, and don't care about the people in the world. Not only is this reviling, but it is slanderous, which the key text mentions as well: "shall say all manner of evil against you falsely".

If the world can't find something to pin on you negatively, they have no problem making something up. In fact, I have recognized a new way that the world is turning people against Christians. As I open my computer for work in the morning, my internet browser gives me some breaking news stories. It should be no secret that there are Christians all around the world who are making the world a better place. They build orphanages and schools, medical centers and shelters, yet we never see these stories. The only stories pertaining to Christians that I see on mainstream media is, for instance, A minister of forty years is arrested for sexually assaulting young women. Another might be 'Hateful' anti-LGBTQ graduation speech at Ohio high school sparks outrage (both were on my page this morning!).

Everywhere you look there is reviling and slander of the one who follows Christ. Nowhere do we see the many more men and women of God who are walking with the Lord and truly making a difference around the world. People are risking their lives in ministry in countries that aren't even allowed to speak the name of Jesus. Others have left comfortable lives to live in a country far away from their friends and family to give the gospel and help people in need.

The Bible tells us to watch out if everyone speaks well of us. Something is wrong if a Christian is well-spoken of in all circles. "Woe unto you, when all men shall speak well of you! for so did their fathers to the false prophets." (Luke 6:26) The world spoke well of the false prophets. Again, the world loves those who imitate Christ, but they are not fond of one who will truly stand up for Truth.

Persecution often gets us out of our comfort zones, leads us to Christ, and helps us to stand up for Him even more.

What about happiness? How can the people around me talking evil of me, hurting me, and even telling lies about me bring happiness? There are two ways. First, it is positional. Because you are being persecuted you must have fruit of a true Christian, and you are blessed because "[yours] is the kingdom of heaven." (Matthew 5:10) You surely have a home in heaven. You surely have power on earth. You surely have access to the Father. You surely have within you the Holy Spirit of God. You surely have the ministry of reconciliation. You surely have the opportunity to make a difference in this world. You surely have the hope, peace, love, and joy that the world needs. You are blessed! The question is do you think on those things and count yourself as blessed or do you see things according to the world? "This I say therefore, and testify in the Lord, that ye henceforth walk not as other Gentiles walk, in the vanity of their mind, Having the understanding darkened, being alienated from the life of God through the ignorance that is in them, because of the blindness of their heart:" (Ephesians 4:17-18)

So, we have that positional happiness that is found in Christ, as with all these beatitudes. Also, however, we have happiness from seeing other people come to the Lord and join the family of God. Again, it is in times of the hottest persecution that we have witnessed the greatest growth in the kingdom of God. That has been the pattern throughout history. It is no different in our present time.

How and why? When we rely on Jesus through the persecution or storm, trial or temptation, the fruit of the Spirit will be the outcome in our lives—even with those tough circumstances, out will come love, joy, peace, longsuffering, gentleness, goodness, forgiveness, mercy, and temperance (Galatians 5:22-23). Showing those things when things are going well isn't going to turn heads much. However, when we can have those great responses in the midst of a storm in our lives, we show that something greater is going on. We show the supernatural light of our Savior, and that makes others want that same relationship. Amen!

Right after the beatitudes in Matthew Chapter 5, Jesus teaches us that we are lights in this dark world. We are salt. We make people see God—bring them to a place of thirsting after God's righteousness. "Ye are the salt of the earth: but if the salt have lost his savour, wherewith shall it be salted? it is thenceforth good for nothing, but to be cast out, and to be trodden under foot of men. Ye are the light of the world. A city that is set on an hill cannot be hid. Neither do men light a candle, and put it under a bushel, but on a candlestick; and it giveth light unto all that are in the house. Let your light so shine before men, that they may see your good works, and glorify your Father which is in heaven." (Matthew 5:13-16)

Light shines best in the dark. It is great to have times of joy and plenty. It is awesome to be around fellow Christians and serve the Lord with gladness. Light is plenteous during these times, and it is a great thing, but we can get so used to the light that we take advantage of the light. We can lose our savor as the Scripture before says, and instead of shining brighter for the Lord, we rely on the lights around us and begin to become dim in comfort.

A few things happen when we decide that we only want to be around light—when we are unwilling to be uncomfortable and tell others about the Light. First of all, as I mentioned, our light will dim, and we will lose our flavor. "Wherefore he saith, Awake thou that sleepest, and arise from the dead, and Christ shall give thee light. See then that ye walk circumspectly, not as fools, but as wise, Redeeming the time, because the days are evil. Wherefore be ye not unwise, but understanding what the will of the Lord is." (Ephesians 5:14-17)

Secondly, when the darkness comes (and it will come) it is so much darker because our light isn't as strong as it was before. A dangerous thing can happen at this time. Instead of being persecuted because you are hot for the Lord, you can become celebrated by the world or those in the world because you are seen as just an imitator. People aren't convicted around you any longer, so they don't persecute you with the tongue or physically. This is not where we are supposed to be. "Ye adulterers and adulteresses, know ye not that the friendship of the world is enmity with God? whosoever therefore will be a friend of the world is the enemy of God." (James 4:4)

Persecution, again, is a sign that you have gotten close to the Lord and when people look at you, they see Him. What a blessing in itself! We must keep our lights shining, so we have to spend some time in the dark—around those who don't know Jesus. We also must embrace the trial or temptation as a place to grow and strengthen our hearts or brighten our lights for the Lord. How can we do that? By remaining close the source: the Light Himself. "Then spake Jesus again unto them, saying, I am the light of the world: he that followeth me shall not walk in darkness, but shall have the light of life." (John 8:12)

In Acts 4, we see that the early church received persecution at its inception. Even still, the outcome was that the church grew: "And as they spake unto the people, the priests, and the captain of the temple, and the Sadducees, came upon them, Being grieved that they taught the people, and preached through Jesus the resurrection from the dead. And they laid hands on them, and put them in hold unto the next day: for it was now eventide. Howbeit many of them which heard the word believed; and the number of the men was about five thousand." (Acts 4:1-4)

We are not to hide our lights! Peter and John spoke to the people, and many were grieved. The powerful words of the gospel of Christ pained their hearts and they responded with persecution. That will be the result of some people that we talk to. Yet, notice that others heard and believed—five thousand men, not including women and children.

We are blessed in America today. Our persecutions are not those of the early church, and they are not those of many other countries still today. In this great nation the persecutions that we know are subtle, yet effective. May we not forget that we have an enemy that is more subtle than any other creature (Genesis 3:1). It is his goal to keep the lost blind and to damage the influence of the Christian— even if all he does is have us believe a little lie such as 'my testimony isn't much for the kingdom of God; it doesn't matter if I witness to others.' Why would we think that way? Subtle persecutions, even those fiery darts from the enemy of our souls. "For we wrestle not against flesh and blood, but against principalities, against powers, against the rulers of the darkness of this world, against spiritual wickedness in high places." (Ephesians 6:12)

While some of our brethren will go to jail or even be killed for preaching the gospel, in this great nation, we only have to worry about losing a friend or follower on social media. Someone might say some negative things about us or even make up lies about us, but we are fairly free to share the gospel and generally don't receive much face-to-face persecution. It is often personal feelings that we will be looked down upon, judged, or seem strange to others.

So, as we learn from Peter and John in Acts 4, we have a certain way that we should respond to persecution. Look at what happened next after Peter and John were taken by those men: "And it came to pass on the morrow, that their rulers, and elders, and scribes, And Annas the high priest, and Caiaphas, and John, and Alexander, and as many as were of the kindred of the high priest, were gathered together at Jerusalem. And when they had set them in the midst, they asked, By what power, or by what name, have ye done this? Then Peter, filled with the Holy Ghost, said unto them, Ye rulers of the people, and elders of Israel, If we this day be examined of the good deed done to the impotent man, by what means he is made whole; Be it known unto you all, and to all the people of Israel, that by the name of Jesus Christ of Nazareth, whom ye crucified, whom God raised from the dead, even by him doth this man stand here before you whole. This is the stone which was set at nought of you builders, which is become the head of the corner. Neither is there salvation in any other: for there is none other name under heaven given among men, whereby we must be saved. Now when they saw the boldness of Peter and John, and perceived that they were unlearned and ignorant men, they marvelled; and they took knowledge of them, that they had been with Jesus. And beholding the man which was healed standing with them, they could say nothing against it." (Acts 4:5-14)

1)   **Be humble and submissive when persecuted for righteousness' sake.** It is easy to fight and be prideful. After all, you would be in the right to defend yourself and simply live out your God-given rights. However, as we see with Peter and John, humility

and submissiveness give them no reason to further persecute you. Instead, they are left looking foolish.

2)   **Be filled with the Holy Ghost**. Let go of all your feelings and desires in that moment and allow yourself to be filled with the Holy Spirit. Pray and hear from God, surrender your will, and wait for God to give you the words to say.

3)   **Boldly speak**. Once you are filled with the Spirit of God, say all that He desires to say, preach Jesus to those who are persecuting you, and stand up for truth and righteousness. When all is done, they will find that you did nothing wrong and will walk away marveled, knowing that if nothing else, you spent time with Jesus. Amen.

"Let us not forget: we are a pilgrim church, subject to misunderstanding, to persecution, but a church that walks serene, because it bears the force of love." — Oscar A. Romero, The Violence of Love

"Those who are walking in the righteousness of Christ will be strengthened by persecution and fire, not destroyed. Fire reveals what cannot be destroyed." — T.F. Tenney, The Main Thing-- Is to Keep the Main Thing the Main Thing

"Yet as persecution—even worldwide persecution—ensues against the Church there will be unity that will come, which will only be explainable as a miracle." — Principles Book

~ 8 ~

PART II: BIBLICAL EXAMPLE

Jeremiah, Truth-Giver where there were no truth-seekers

Jeremiah was known as the weeping prophet. He was called by God to deliver a message that the people did not hear. Jeremiah was to tell the people that judgment was coming and that they needed to return to the Lord and surrender to the judgment that was headed their way, which was the nation of Babylon.

Jeremiah was one of the few true prophets in his day, as there were many other prophets, priests, and kings who preached peace and victory over Babylon. The people chose the false prophets over the true prophet, and Jeremiah was mocked, beaten, imprisoned, and eventually killed—persecuted at every level for righteousness' sake.

Some would call Jeremiah's message dark or depressing, just like many people call the Christian's message of judgment dark and depressing, but it was a message of repentance and a message of hope. God told Jeremiah to call the people to repent so that He would be able to have mercy on them again.

Every priest and prophet had the same message—repent —turn to the Lord and away from sin, self and the enemy of our souls. It is the way of salvation, eternally and in our present day in everyday situations. In fact, every beatitude that we've studied thus far gets us to this point that we'd be so aligned with God that our overall message that we speak is repent because God loves you and has made a way for you to get to heaven and have victory over sin in this life.

Again, we start with the attitude that we are poor in spirit—we can do nothing and have nothing truly apart from God—nothing that matters. We have eternal needs that will not be met by the carnal ways that we attempt to receive them, whether it's love, joy, peace, acceptance, purpose...etc. We need God. That attitude of humility is our first step toward a holy and loving God.

As we start to seek God out and recognize how awesome He is, we realize how needy and unworthy we are and it makes us mourn over our sin which creates a gentleness in the way that we deal with others; and as God calls us outside of ourselves, we desire even more of Him and find Him to be our fulfillment in life. Those attitudes open us to minister to others, showing God's mercy to a dying world of darkness as we learn to let go of any impurities so that we can see God clearer and can be peacemakers, turning hearts toward Jesus, the One who brings peace.

Jeremiah, no doubt, exhibited these attitudes. God called him from a young age, according to Jeremiah Chapter 1: "Then the word of the LORD came unto me, saying, Before I formed thee in the belly I knew thee; and before thou camest forth out of the womb I sanctified thee, and I ordained thee a prophet unto the nations. Then said I, Ah, Lord GOD! behold, I cannot speak: for I am a child. But the LORD said unto me, Say not, I am a child: for thou shalt go to all that I shall send thee, and whatsoever I command thee thou shalt speak. Be not afraid of their faces: for I am with thee to deliver thee, saith the LORD. Then the LORD put forth his hand, and touched my mouth. And the LORD said unto me, Behold, I have put my words in thy mouth. See, I have this day set thee over the nations and over the kingdoms, to root out, and to pull down, and to destroy, and to throw down, to build, and to plant." (Jeremiah 1:4-10)

Jeremiah's mission was clear: Go and do and say what I tell you. God had a plan for him and would lead him to and through it, just like God has a plan for each of us. "For I know the thoughts that I think toward you, saith the Lord, thoughts of peace, and not of evil, to give you an expected end." (Jeremiah 29:11) Also similar to each one of our callings, Jeremiah was told not to be afraid because God was with Him every step of the way. "Go ye therefore, and teach all nations, baptizing them in the name of the Father, and of the Son, and of the Holy Ghost: Teaching them to observe all things whatsoever I have commanded you: and, lo, I am with you alway, even unto the end of the world. Amen." (Matthew 28:19-20)

Jeremiah suffered great heartache because of the rebellion of the people, knowing that their hard-heartedness would lead many of them to never see the promised land again, including his king. He hid as they burned the Scriptures, unwilling to share the truth with the people. (Scripture) He was set outside in stocks in front of the temple like a criminal (Scripture), and thrown into a dungeon more than once and left for dead. (Scriptures)

Even after Jeremiah's prophesy proved true when Babylon was able to sweep through Jerusalem, destroying the land and taking many captive, Jeremiah was faced with more persecution. The people who remained in Jerusalem went to him claiming to desire truth. They asked Jeremiah to go to God on their behalf so that they would know what to do next. "Then they said to Jeremiah, The LORD be a true and faithful witness between us, if we do not even according to all things for the which the LORD thy God shall send thee to us. Whether it be good, or whether it be evil, we will obey the voice of the LORD our God, to whom we send thee; that it may be well with us, when we obey the voice of the LORD our God." (Jeremiah 42:5-6)

After ten days God responded to Jeremiah and gave them the message not to go to Egypt. They were told that Egypt would be the end of them. However, God promised mercy and deliverance if they remained and trusted in Him though it didn't make sense. Did they obey the voice of the Lord? Did they count God's witness to be true?

Their response: "And it came to pass, that when Jeremiah had made an end of speaking unto all the people all the words of the LORD their God, for which the LORD their God had sent him to them, even all these words, Then spake Azariah the son of Hoshaiah, and Johanan the son of Kareah, and all the proud men, saying unto Jeremiah, Thou speakest falsely: the LORD our God hath not sent thee to say, Go not into Egypt to sojourn there:" (Jeremiah 43:1-2)

They sadly did the opposite of what the Lord commanded and kidnapped Jeremiah and took him with them to Egypt (Jeremiah 43:5-6) where tradition and church history says they eventually stoned him to death.

Jeremiah's story doesn't seem like a happy one. He even considered quitting—giving up— at one point, but His heart toward the Lord wouldn't let him: "O LORD, thou hast deceived me, and I was deceived: thou art stronger than I, and hast prevailed: I am in derision daily, every one mocketh me. For since I spake, I cried out, I cried violence and spoil; because the word of the LORD was made a reproach unto me, and a derision, daily. Then I said, I will not make mention of him, nor speak any more in his name. But his word was in mine heart as a burning fire shut up in my bones, and I was weary with forbearing, and I could not stay. For I heard the defaming of many, fear on every side. Report, say they, and we will report it. All my familiars watched for my halting, saying, Peradventure he will be enticed, and we shall prevail against him, and we shall take our revenge on him. But the LORD is with me as a mighty terrible one: therefore my persecutors shall stumble, and they shall not prevail: they shall be greatly ashamed; for they shall not prosper: their everlasting confusion shall never be forgotten." (Jeremiah 20:7-11)

Even though Jeremiah was a hated peacemaker who was persecuted for righteousness' sake, he had purpose. Quitting would've been easy. In fact, it is often made clear that one is not a true believer when it comes down to whether one will suffer with

Christ for Christ. Jeremiah said the Word of God was a reproach and derision daily. Every day he felt disapproval and mockery from those around him. Yet, when he tried to quit, all he could think about was the Word of God and he could not be quiet. Why? People needed the truth. Many wanted him to quit; however, they would've been without another opportunity to turn to the Lord. Besides, he realized, God was stronger than anything that they could bring on him and the Lord had delivered him time and time again out of the people's hands. Ultimately, God is judge and for those who go against Him and His people, there will be a great judgment.

Jeremiah may have thought that not a single soul heard him. He may have had many of discouraging days and nights. However, Jeremiah couldn't know that there was a remnant of young men that would keep God's Word alive, even through the Babylonian captivity, led by a great man named Daniel.

Daniel would've been a boy at the height of Jeremiah's ministry and, no doubt, would've seen and heard some of Jeremiah's messages. Jeremiah wrote of the 70-year reign of Babylon in Jeremiah 25, which is said to be the same year that Daniel and his friends, Ananiah, Azariah, and Mishael were taken captive by Babylon. It was also likely that Daniel was the one who received the letter that Jeremiah wrote to Babylon eight years later—the same letter and Scripture that Daniel read to Cyrus, king of the Medes, that got Cyrus to release those taken captive by the Babylonians.

How amazing is that! We won't always see the fruit of our continued work for the Lord. We won't always get to eat of the abundance of His feast while on earth, but one thing is for sure and that is that the suffering that we have on earth is nothing compared to the glory that we will have in heaven—suffering for days while glory for millennia. "For I reckon that the sufferings of this present time are not worthy to be compared with the glory which shall be revealed in us." (Romans 8:18)

Happiness is not just about how I feel right now. Happiness comes from having purpose and vision in life. Happiness comes from helping others and making a difference. No person who lived for themselves and had all they ever wanted ever claimed happiness at the end of their lives. They had regrets. How do I know that? Because the Word of God tells me and you that happiness comes from knowing God and living for Him. We can't fool ourselves too long. It's the reason why so many rich and famous people who could have anything they want are miserable.

Jeremiah even told us "Blessed is the man that trusteth in the LORD, and whose hope the LORD is. For he shall be as a tree planted by the waters, and that spreadeth out her roots by the river, and shall not see when heat cometh, but her leaf shall be green; and shall not be careful in the year of drought, neither shall cease from yielding fruit." (Jeremiah 17:7-8)

Blessed or happy is the one who trusts in God and makes God their hope because they will be well-nourished and even when the hard times come, they will be in a place of growth and will still be fruitful. That will be any of us who, through persecutions and sufferings, trust God. When we know God well enough to have a confident expectation that everything is going to work out, we will be happy in the calling that He gives us, even if, like Jeremiah, it's a hard one, which is the likelihood because God wants us to be uncomfortable and need to rely on the Comforter, His Holy Spirit.

Have you allowed yourself to grow in the Lord to a place where people are starting to not like you because of your zeal for the Lord? It is promised that all who live godly will suffer persecution. (2 Timothy 3:12) It is a mark of one who has gotten to the place where they love God more than self. Wow!

We can look around and see that the last days are here and many love themselves rather than God. They will mock and curse, belittle and defame any who show themselves godly. Yet, that shows the more that they need Jesus. Will we let the Word be shut up in us or be like Jeremiah unable to be quiet because we love God and we love people?

~ 8 ~

PART II: BIBLICAL EXAMPLE

Paul, from persecutor to persecuted

In chapter 4, we took a brief look at Paul and how his desires changed from religious zealot to humble follower of Christ. There are a lot of differences between Paul and Jeremiah. While Jeremiah got his call as a young boy, it wasn't until Paul was about 30 that he received his call from the Lord. Jeremiah preached in the day of the law, while Paul preached in the day of grace. Jeremiah likely never knew of any converts under his ministry, while Paul witnessed many lives changed, with his faithfulness being charged.

However, the two men also had something in common. They both heard the call of the Lord and followed it, and because of that, they were persecuted for righteousness' sake.

As we looked at before, Paul was a persecutor of believers before he became a follower of Christ. He was a zealot for the Law, the Old Testament way of living—the keeping of ordinances, feasts and, of course, the Law. He mentions in several of his epistles how he persecuted the church: "Circumcised the eighth day, of the stock of Israel, of the tribe of Benjamin, an Hebrew of the Hebrews; as touching the law, a Pharisee; Concerning zeal, persecuting the church; touching the righteousness which is in the law, blameless." (Philippians 3:5-6) "For ye have heard of my conversation in time past in the Jews' religion, how that beyond measure I persecuted the church of God, and wasted it: And profited in the Jews' religion above many my equals in mine own nation, being more exceedingly zealous of the traditions of my fathers." (Galatians 1:13-14)

Paul prided himself in his religion before he had gotten to know Jesus. He would've been proud to say all the things that he did before in persecuting the church, but when he speaks of it, he is vague, no doubt feeling shame for the way he treated what were at the point of writing those epistles brothers and sisters in Christ.

As Luke writes Acts, he goes into more detail about the persecutions by Paul, even recording some of Paul's words: "I am verily a man which am a Jew, born in Tarsus, a city in Cilicia, yet brought up in this city at the feet of Gamaliel, and taught according to the perfect manner of the law of the fathers, and was zealous toward God, as ye all are this day. And I persecuted this way unto the death, binding and delivering into prisons both men and women. As also the high priest doth bear me witness, and all the estate of the elders: from whom also I received letters unto the brethren, and went to Damascus, to bring them which were there bound unto Jerusalem, for to be punished." (Acts 22:3-5)

Paul went on to describe meeting Jesus on his way to Damascus to further persecute the church. "And it came to pass, that, as I made my journey, and was come nigh unto Damascus about noon, suddenly there shone from heaven a great light round about me. And I fell unto the ground, and heard a voice saying unto me, Saul, Saul, why persecutest thou me? And I answered, Who art thou, Lord? And he said unto me, I am Jesus of Nazareth, whom thou persecutest. And they that were with me saw indeed the light, and were afraid; but they heard not the voice of him that spake to me. And I said, What shall I do, Lord? And the Lord said unto me, Arise, and go into Damascus; and there it shall be told thee of all things which are appointed for thee to do." (Acts 22:6-10)

That is when Paul received his calling from God to share the gospel with the Gentiles—those nations that were without God. Paul answered that call with sincerity and never looked back. He is possibly the greatest missionary that ever lived. He is most certainly the very first.

Paul could've let his past deter him from doing great things for God, but he immediately went about the Lord's business. "And when he had received meat, he was strengthened. Then was Saul certain days with the disciples which were at Damascus. And straightway he preached Christ in the synagogues, that he is the Son of God." (Acts 9:19-20)

Paul was in a place of stature and comfort, no doubt, when he got the call from Jesus to go preach the gospel. He probably thought himself to be "happy." He was fulfilling what he thought was his dream job in a high position in the court of religious leaders. He had authority that others didn't have. Because of his stature, rank, education opportunities, travel, and influence, it can be inferred that he was a wealthy man, although often Paul chose to go without.

However, he traded the world's happiness for the high calling of God in Christ Jesus, a more generous and everlasting happiness. Paul esteemed the position of child of God over every human position that supposedly brings happiness.

Let us remember that God is much more concerned with our present and future than our past. Paul is an excellent example of what the Lord can do in a heart and life. When Paul turned from his old life and answered the call of Jesus, those who were afraid of him were soon amazed at his teaching and preaching and grew in the Lord; however, those close friends of his, acquaintances, teachers, and "co-workers," wanted him dead: "But all that heard him were amazed, and said; Is not this he that destroyed them which called on this name in Jerusalem, and came hither for that intent, that he might bring them bound unto the chief priests? But Saul increased the more in strength, and confounded the Jews which dwelt at Damascus, proving that this is very Christ. And after that many days were fulfilled, the Jews took counsel to kill him:" (Acts 9:21-23)

He escaped many times, but he did have to go through many persecutions. He was thrown out of cities, stoned, went without food, drink, clothing and shelter, beaten, jailed, and left for dead more than once. Paul recognized these persecutions as part of the life of those who are truly following Christ. As false preachers preached against him and brought a "different" gospel to the people, Paul admonished the people, "Are they ministers of Christ? (I speak as a fool) I am more; in labours more abundant, in stripes above measure, in prisons more frequent, in deaths oft. Of the Jews five times received I forty stripes save one. Thrice was I beaten with rods, once was I stoned, thrice I suffered shipwreck, a night and a day I have been in the deep; In journeyings often, in perils of waters, in perils of robbers, in perils by mine own countrymen, in perils by the heathen, in perils in the city, in perils in the wilderness, in perils in the sea, in perils among false brethren; In weariness and painfulness, in watchings often, in hunger and thirst, in fastings often, in cold and nakedness. Beside those things that are without, that which cometh upon me daily, the care of all the churches. Who is weak, and I am not weak? who is offended, and I burn not? If I must needs glory, I will glory of the things which concern mine infirmities." (2 Corinthians 11:23-30)

Those false teachers were claiming that Paul was weak, insinuating that he didn't have the power of God on him. Paul inferred that because he had gone through so much, they could count him true, and, even more, they could count God true as He got him through all of those persecutions to come out even stronger.

Every place where you read of Paul being persecuted, you read of people coming to know the Lord. Paul is known for three missionary journeys where the gospel was spread throughout the eastern world. He preached and planted churches. He mentored others and developed them into leaders.

Unlike Jeremiah, Paul saw much fruit of his faithfulness in the Lord, yet there was no lack of tears on the part of Paul. Surely, he desired to see even more come to know the Savior; however, he had no regrets at the end of his life. Sensing that his death was eminent, Paul wrote, "For I am now ready to be offered, and the time of my departure is at hand. I have fought a good fight, I have finished my course, I have kept the faith: Henceforth there is laid up for me a crown of righteousness, which the Lord, the righteous judge, shall give me at that day: and not to me only, but unto all them also that love his appearing." (2 Timothy 4:6-8)

What a testimony! What a great understanding of God's purpose and calling! What great happiness can be seen as Paul looks forward even to taking his last breath. He was martyred for his faith, as most believe, by Nero, beheaded after the great fires in around 64AD. I have no doubt that even still Paul smiles down as people are surrendering to the Lord and growing in the Lord because of his ministry today.

I am not so mature in my faith that I always recognize persecution through Jesus' eyes. I don't always see the blessing in it. I certainly don't always see the purpose in it, but I am learning to see both. God grows us as we get into His Word more, and while these concepts are foreign and even go against our natural way of thinking, they are God's ways, and they build His kingdom.

~ 8 ~

PART III: PERSONAL EXAMPLE

The first time that I ever received persecution was in my home. I had gone to church for only two weeks, but God was doing a work on my heart. Reading and studying my Bible, going to church and spending more time with people who loved the Lord had brought hope back into my thoughts and feelings, and as I went through my days at home, I began to express that hope in words and actions.

I remember, clearly, the spiritual battle between my then-boyfriend and me. He said many hurtful words, rejecting my faith and often even God Himself. As I was hopeful for our future, he was still making plans to leave.

I call this persecution because, without going into detail, I was provoked to walk away from God. I was provoked to live for myself and engage in things that I had already put away because of my pregnancy. I was not only provoked but mistreated for my belief in Jesus. Let's recall, though, that persecution has purpose.

There is a choice to be made when we are persecuted. We quickly find out if our faith is real or not. "And these are they likewise which are sown on stony ground; who, when they have heard the Word, immediately receive it with gladness; And have no root in themselves, and so endure but for a time: afterward, when affliction or persecution ariseth for the word's sake, immediately they are offended. And these are they which are sown among thorns; such as hear the Word, And the cares of this world, and the deceitfulness of riches, and the lusts of other things entering in, choke the Word, and it becometh unfruitful." (Mark 4:16-19)

My troubles at home drew me closer to God, His Word, and His people. It wasn't long that my now-husband joined me, got saved, and is now preaching the Word of God. Happiness came from withstanding that persecution. Fruit came from enduring.

As I mentioned, my house was a go-to for family gatherings, and I had a hard time balancing my faith with my extended family. I wanted to be a witness to them, but I realized that most of them thought I had two different lives until I began to stand my ground and not allow some of the former things in my home any longer. Unfortunately, that is when the time of family gatherings at my home became less and less. However, I was still influencing my family. There were very few people in my immediate circle that didn't go to church at least once from one of my invites, and many proclaimed salvation.

After about a year and a half to two years, I believe it became apparent to people that I was really a new person. I hadn't just "caught religion." Jesus won my heart, and family gatherings became harder to attend. I overheard people talking about me and my family. It was obvious that we were going different directions, and though my love never changed for my extended family, our fellowship was different, which made them believe my love was different.

I'll never forget that a sister of mine came to visit one day. We had been estranged really most of our lives. She and I have the same father but different mothers. We grew up in different households and different cities and states. She told me there was an obvious change in me, and she wanted to have that change in herself.

I found it amazing that she had heard things about me. Not everyone reported to her in the most positive ways, as she said that she heard that I was in a cult. I found that funny. Either way, people were talking about me and my faith and because of that my sister and I became closer than we had ever been before. We still talk regularly, and I hope to be a positive example in her life as she is one in my life.

Talk of me being in a cult, though, is a form of persecution. I had heard whispers of family members thinking the same thing, but it never turned me away from God. I find it sad that our world is so lukewarm concerning true Christianity that when a person truly gets on fire for God, he/she is considered to be in some sort of cult. What a great day it will be when more Christians live Christ-like so that we can more readily spot those who are frauds and thieves instead of Christ-like people getting the bad rep. Then again, how did the people treat Jesus?

Loss of familial relationships and friendships were my most hurtful persecutions, and while they weren't violent or extreme, they could've drawn me away from God if I wasn't watchful and stayed doing what I knew to be right.

My most public persecutions have been on YouTube videos that I have done. I never really expect many people to watch videos that I produce, and certainly not people that I don't know, yet I have had people respond to videos in the comments with unnecessarily negative comments. It is persecution because it is obvious from my title of the video that the person shouldn't have even watched the video because it was against their views; yet they watched it and commented. I used such instances as an opportunity to teach and even preach. I have been able to have some tough conversations that I wouldn't have otherwise had with people that I would have never otherwise spoken to, so it turned out to be a blessing, although I'm sure we all went our own ways with the same opinions. Who knows how God can use moments like that.

Other than those, I have had very light persecutions while going to give out tracts or invite people to church. People said no, sometimes aggressively. Overall, however, I have been blessed as I followed God's calling.

Presently, there is an atmospheric change in America. The political climate has gotten harsh toward Christians and anyone who will stand up for Truth. It won't be long, unfortunately, that this great nation will see harsher persecution.

The question for all of us must be: are we ready? Are we ready for the persecutions that will come for us because we choose to stand with God?

$$\sim 8 \sim$$

PART IV: GO DEEPER

1. What does it mean to be persecuted?

----

2. What are Christians persecuted for?

----

3. What are some of the reasons that a Christian should be happy when persecuted for righteousness' sake?

----

4. Read Job Chapter 1 and answer the following questions:
a. Was Job a righteous man?

----

b. How was he blessed by God?

----

c. Who was allowed to tempt him?

----

d. What does that tell us about persecution and the Christian?

----

e. Does God tempt us? (see also James 1:13)

----

f. Does God allow temptation?

----

5. Why do you think God allows temptation? (See also James 1:2-12 "My brethren, count it all joy when ye fall into divers temptations; Knowing this, that the trying of your faith worketh patience. But let patience have her perfect work, that ye may be perfect and entire, wanting nothing. If any of you lack wisdom, let him ask of God, that giveth to all men liberally, and upbraideth not; and it shall be given him. But let him ask in faith, nothing wavering. For he that wavereth is like a wave of the sea driven with the wind and tossed. For let not that man think that he shall receive any thing of the Lord. A double minded man is unstable in all his ways. Let the brother of low degree rejoice in that he is exalted: But the rich, in that he is made low: because as the flower of the grass he shall pass away. For the sun is no sooner risen with a burning heat, but it withereth the grass, and the flower thereof falleth, and the grace of the fashion of it perisheth: so also shall the rich man fade away in his ways. Blessed is the man that endureth temptation: for when he is tried, he shall receive the crown of life, which the Lord hath promised to them that love him." (James 1:2-12)

----

6. How does what we learned in this chapter and the last chapter reconcile with a lot of modern Christian teaching that if you walk with God, everything will be perfect? Is that Biblical? Why or why not? Write at least one Scripture to support your answer.

----

7. It's easy to get discouraged and look at things from our own mindset instead of that of the Lord. In doing so, we may forget that we are blessed when we are persecuted. How can the verses below give you hope and put your mind back on Jesus?

"Blessed be the God and Father of our Lord Jesus Christ, which according to his abundant mercy hath begotten us again unto a lively hope by the resurrection of Jesus Christ from the dead, To an inheritance incorruptible, and undefiled, and that fadeth not away, reserved in heaven for you, Who are kept by the power of God through faith unto salvation ready to be revealed in the last time. Wherein ye greatly rejoice, though now for a season, if need be, ye are in heaviness through manifold temptations: That the trial of your faith, being much more precious than of gold that perisheth, though it be tried with fire, might be found unto praise and honour and glory at the appearing of Jesus Christ:" (1 Peter 1:3-7)

----

8. How could the verses below help you in such times of persecution?

a. 1 Corinthians 10:13

---

b. 1 Peter 5:10

---

c. John 16:33

---

d. Philippians 4:6-8

---

e. 1 Peter 4:12

---

f. Romans 8:28

---

g. Psalms 34:17-18

---

h. 2 Corinthians 12:9

---

9. What should we do if we face persecution?

____

____

____

____

____

____

~ 9 ~

PSYCHOLOGY AND HAPPINESS

Do the "experts" agree with the Bible?

God's ways are always the best ways. Even some "experts" agree with what the Bible says about happiness. For instance, a writer for Psychology Today defines happiness as "a state of well-being that encompasses living a good life, one with a sense of meaning and deep contentment."[4] It has been realized that it is more than just a "positive mood."

Perhaps you picked up this book and had no interest in the Lord or Biblical values and principles but you are desperate for happiness. I wonder if one without the Lord can truly ever be happy, even from the definition used above. We would all have to define a "good life," and surely we'd have different definitions.

Then, we'd have to look at what meaning in life could be. Does one without God have meaning in life?

What about contentment—deep contentment? Would we all agree what contentment is? I believe this is probably the most concrete of the words above but the world's definition of contentment is still lacking. Contentment is defined as a state of happiness or satisfaction. Biblically, contentment is being satisfied with what you have. "Let your conversation be without covetousness; and be content with such things as ye have: for he hath said, I will never leave thee, nor forsake thee." (Hebrews 13:5) The source of contentment is God and a trust in Him.

According to Psychology today, which we can all agree with, finding happiness is a global pursuit. We all want it, no matter where we are from. We would also agree that happiness is not without troubles. Life is not perfect for anyone in any season. We will have hard times, but we can have happiness in hard times because it is about our attitude in those times more than anything else.

Like the Bible, the "experts" claim that "research shows that much of happiness is under personal control." In this book we looked at eight attitudes that bring lifelong happiness. I found that the psychologists who have created an entire science of happiness called positive psychology also have those keys to lasting happiness: "The key to lifelong happiness is taking time to cultivate small tweaks on a regular basis. Incorporating habits into your daily life such as keeping a gratitude journal, practicing kindness, nurturing optimism, learning to forgive, investing in relationships, finding flow activities, avoiding overthinking, savoring life's joys, and committing to goals can make happiness a permanent fixture."[5]

Can I say that it seems as if Christianity is the epitome of happiness, even according to the "experts." The first thing mentioned is to take time to change up if needed. The Bible tells us many places to consider ourselves and examine ourselves and to make sure we are walking in the right way. "Ponder the path of thy feet, and let all thy ways be established." (Proverbs 14:26)

"Examine yourselves, whether ye be in the faith; prove your own selves. Know ye not your own selves, how that Jesus Christ is in you, except ye be reprobates?" (2 Corinthians 13:5)

It should be the daily process of every Christian to evaluate their steps and readjust if they have gotten off-course.

Next, in the article referenced above, the writer goes on to give practical things that one can do to have lifelong happiness: "keeping a gratitude journal, practicing kindness, nurturing optimism, learning to forgive, investing in relationships, finding flow activities, avoiding overthinking, savoring life's joys, and committing to goals can make happiness a permanent fixture."

Keep a gratitude journal—The Word of God tells us to remember God and all His goodness to us.

"Bless the LORD, O my soul, and forget not all his benefits:" (Psalm 103:2)

To remember is one of the ordinances of God that Jesus left for us to do: ""And he took bread, and gave thanks, and brake it, and gave unto them, saying, This is my body which is given for you: this do in remembrance of me." (Luke 22:19)

What a great way to remember by writing it down in a journal.

- Practicing kindness—This is another command from God to the Christian.

"And be ye kind one to another, tenderhearted, forgiving one another, even as God for Christ's sake hath forgiven you." (Ephesians 4:32)

- Nurturing optimism—The Word of God implores all His people to think positively.

"Finally, brethren, whatsoever things are true, whatsoever things are honest, whatsoever things are just, whatsoever things are pure, whatsoever things are lovely, whatsoever things are of good report; if there be any virtue, and if there be any praise, think on these things." (Philippians 4:8)

Learning to forgive—We saw this above in Ephesians 4:32 as a part of kindness, but it is also a commandment that we can know the forgiveness of God.

"For if ye forgive men their trespasses, your heavenly Father will also forgive you: But if ye forgive not men their trespasses, neither will your Father forgive your trespasses." (Matthew 6:14-15)

It is a heart thing. If we stop forgiving others, we forget that God, because of Jesus, has forgiven us and we find ourselves walking in darkness. However, we don't have to remain there because if we take that to God and agree that we were wrong, we can receive that forgiveness and cleansing: "If we confess our sins, he is faithful and just to forgive us our sins, and to cleanse us from all unrighteousness." (1 John 1:9)

- Investing in relationships—One of the marks of a Christian is one who is welcoming and hospitable. It is by relationships that we can share the gospel with others that they can see how good God is.

"And above all things have fervent charity among yourselves: for charity shall cover the multitude of sins. Use hospitality one to another without grudging. As every man hath received the gift, even so minister the same one to another, as good stewards of the manifold grace of God." (1 Peter 4:8-10)

- Finding flow activities—A flow activity is an activity that is challenging and rewarding, that works toward a goal. This is a great thing to do toward happiness, and it is what every Christian should be doing. We are to engage in the activity of sharing the gospel, being a light to our community.

"Go ye therefore, and teach all nations, baptizing them in the name of the Father, and of the Son, and of the Holy Ghost: Teaching them to observe all things whatsoever I have commanded you: and, lo, I am with you alway, even unto the end of the world. Amen." (Matthew 28:19-20)

There is a goal to see the kingdom of God built, lives changed and God receiving honor and glory that He is so worthy of.

- Avoiding overthinking—While I certainly have not mastered this, I know where my problem in it is: I rely on my own way of thinking, which causes me to overthink. The Word of God tells us to trust in the Lord, and trusting God relieves overthinking.

"Trust in the LORD with all thine heart; and lean not unto thine own understanding. In all thy ways acknowledge him, and he shall direct thy paths." (Proverbs 3:5-6)

Savoring life's joys—This to me is saying be thankful, which is missing from this list but is definitely a component of happiness—lasting happiness. It is also a commandment from God.

"Rejoice in the Lord alway: and again I say, Rejoice. Let your moderation be known unto all men. The Lord is at hand. Be careful for nothing; but in every thing by prayer and supplication with thanksgiving let your requests be made known unto God. And the peace of God, which passeth all understanding, shall keep your hearts and minds through Christ Jesus." (Philippians 4:4-7)

- Committing to goals—To have goals is to look forward, not backward. It is to make an active choice to continue to work on something until you've reached the finish line of that project. All Christians have been given an order to continuously march forward with the goal of bringing God glory by becoming more and more like His Son. Though it is assumed, no Christian considers himself/herself perfect. We are always growing, though. We have put forth the goals that God has laid out in His Word.

"Brethren, I count not myself to have apprehended: but this one thing I do, forgetting those things which are behind, and reaching forth unto those things which are before, I press toward the mark for the prize of the high calling of God in Christ Jesus." (Philippians 3:13-14)

Many psychologists even understand that there is a spiritual part to this happiness that we all desire. They may not choose a "god" for anyone or claim that any god is above another, but they do state that religion or spirituality does contribute to happiness. One article put it this way: "Spirituality and religion also have the capacity to create joy, community, and meaning. Abiding by the values of a given religion, which often include community, self-care, and a trusting relationship with God, can help individuals find health and happiness."[6]

That same article goes on to say: "Research has revealed a strong link between psychological well-being and religion and spirituality. There are also connections to better health, such as lower rates of smoking and alcohol use, better sleep, and even a longer lifespan. Yet there are elements of religions that can cause distress in some cases, such as feelings of guilt or shame."[7]

Of course, all religions are not equal. There is only one faith and that is faith in the Son of God, Jesus Christ who died for our sins, was buried and rose the third day in victory over sin, death, and the enemy of our souls. With Him, there is no guilt or shame because He removes it all through a personal relationship with Him.

FOOTNOTES

1. Websters 1828 dictionary

2. You can also read about Nebuchadnezzar and his kingdom in 2 Kings 24-25, 2 Chronicles 36, and Jeremiah 21-52

3. www.biblehistory.net/newsletter/nebuchadnezzar.htm

4. www.psychologytoday.com/us/basics/happiness

5. www.psychologytoday.com/us/basics/happiness

6. www.psychologytoday.com/us/basics/happiness/the-science-happiness

7. www.psychologytoday.com/us/basics/happiness/the-science-happiness

www.ingramcontent.com/pod-product-compliance
Lightning Source LLC
Chambersburg PA
CBHW071413150726

48000CB00001B/306